Golf Fitness: Shed Pounds to Shave Strokes

Drive the Fat Out of Your Game for Lower Scores

By Christian Henning, NASM-CPT, gfs
Photography by Richard Guzzo

To my Dad and Grandfather,

Thank you for introducing me to the greatest game of them all.

Table of Contents

STOP! DO THIS NOW.

As one of the Shed Pounds to Shave Strokes bonuses, you get FREE support via Facebook, Twitter, and Email.

Using our Facebook fan page has proven to help our clients lose fat faster and stick to your diet and workout program. That's where you'll get positive social support from people from all over the World. You can even ask Christian Henning, the author of Shed Pounds to Shave Strokes, all of your diet and exercise questions.

Here's how to get the most value and SUCCESS from your purchase of this book. Take care of these now, and ask a question so you can get in the habit of letting us coach you to the golf body of your dreams.

Step 1 - Join our Facebook Community @ facebook.com/getfitforgolf

Step 2 - Join us on Twitter @ twitter.com/GetFitForGolf

Step 3 - Go to golff.it/printable to claim your Shed Pounds to Shave Strokes printable content. I created so much content I couldn't pack it all in to one book because it would be too large! You can download a Goal Planning Guide, Diet Guide, Pre-Round Warm Up Guide, and Printable Workout Sheets by entering your email in the link.

Step 4 - Enter the golfbodychallenge.com. This is our transformation contest that runs three times a year and gives away cash and prizes.

Please let us know if you have any questions about using the Shed Pounds to Shave Strokes workout program.

Other Golf Fitness Books by Christian Henning

Golf Fitness: 30 Yards or More in 30 Days or Less

30 Yards or More in 30 Days or Less is the workout to do AFTER Shed Pounds to Shave Strokes. This more advanced program to begin immediately after Shed Pounds is our core strengthening and power workout program.

This 4-week (advanced) to 8-week (Intermediate and beginner) workout program is designed to build on the base you create in Shed Pounds to Shave Strokes. In a nutshell, this is a tour pro caliber workout designed to improve golf performance and provide you with more distance, stamina, and control.

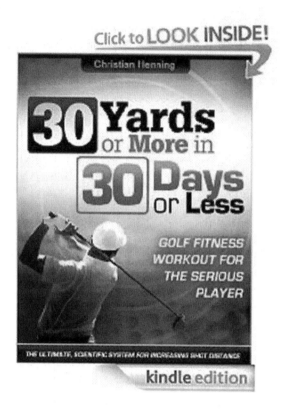

Get Your Copy Here: ==> http://golff.it/30in30

- Build Balance, Flexibility, Strength, and Power in just 30 days
- Dumbbells, Stability Ball, and a Chair are all you need.
- Beginner, Intermediate, and Advanced Workouts included.

Chapter One: What 'They' Don't Want You To Know

I need you to forget the myth that long sessions of cardio are the most important aspects of a fat loss program.

Cardio manufacturers don't want you to know what I'm going to reveal below. And why should they? The more machines they sell, the more money they make. Don't get me wrong, I am glad the equipment is made - but disagree with the methods prescribed for these machines that is commonly accepted to burn fat. Essentially, long and slow cardio doesn't burn fat as efficiently as the Interval training we implement in our workout program.

Science is behind me on this one.. So don't believe the hype!

While cardio machines are used in our program, we use them differently than the accepted norm. Why? Because the accepted norm doesn't work for burning fat in the optimal and most time efficient manner. But more about this and the concept and science behind Shed Pounds to Shave Strokes is below…

What are the secrets to a workout that improves golf performance, while burning fat at the same time?

Shed Pounds to Shave Strokes utilizes 'Turbulence Training' and 'Translation Training' to keep your body in an ever adapting state. Through forced adaptation, we force the body to burn fat and improve golf performance. For maximum results, we will be applying these principles to your body in both weight training and in short burst cardio sessions.

We will use the Turbulence method in our Interval workouts (cardio) and Translation Training method in our weight training to improve our golf performance.

Turbulence burns the fat off. Translation Training builds a powerful golf body.

A good analogy for Turbulence is that of a car starting and stopping. The more starting and stopping the car does, the more fuel is burned. When the car is on the highway at a constant speed, less fuel is burned.

Now consider long boring cardio sessions that last anywhere from 45 minutes to an hour. Generally, people keep the same pace over these long periods. Think highway cruising…

Less fuel burned.

To improve our golf performance, we will be applying Translation Training to your muscles. Essentially, we will be mimicking the movements that create balance, strength and power in your golf swing.

Turbulence and Translation Training by design put a huge amount of "Metabolic Disturbance" on your muscles. After your workouts, your muscles will work very hard (burning calories) to return your body to normal. That's how both principles combine to help you lose fat and sculpt your body through proven our proven methods.

You will find bursting through fat loss plateaus becomes much easier using these principles. Most of the programs you may be familiar with are high-volume, low-intensity, and don't stress the muscle the same way our workouts will. So if you are currently using long, slow, boring cardio and begin using the Shed Pounds to Shave Strokes

workouts, you have a potent stimulus to kick-start fat loss –
no matter how stubborn it was in the past.

I've created a progressive program for you that will get you
moving and give you over 12-weeks of workouts. Whether
you are a beginner or advanced, you can jump right in and
see results instantly.

Beginners need to start with the Beginner program. Don't
try to attempt the Intermediate or Advanced workouts. The
programs are designed to be followed in order and will
prepare you for the next set of workouts.

Intermediate and Advanced are for those who have been
working out awhile. Even if you think you are super fit and
advanced, start with the Intermediate workouts. Quite
simply, the new Intervals will be quite difficult if done
properly. Don't get ahead of yourself.

Shed Pounds to Shave Strokes is for busy people.
Workouts only require a maximum of 45 minutes 3 times
per week. Efficient and effective workouts with clear
purposes: Improve golf performance and burn fat.

Surely you have 45 minutes 3 times a week to achieve
your goals?

Variety. Intensity. Change.

These principles are the cornerstone of our fat loss program and have been proven in research labs around the World. Keeping the workouts fresh, changing them every four weeks, and applying the proper intensity will keep you on track.

If we were perform the same workouts month after month, your body would not be forced to adapt. Thus, we would get minimal to no results. You would become used to the work and your body would not be forced to adapt. This is why we change the program every four weeks.

In order to keep losing fat and gain muscle, you must change the program periodically. This is done by changing the number of sets, reps, types of exercises, and other variables to force adaptation.

Some beginners may be able to keep adapting up to 12 weeks before their progress starts to reach a point of diminishing returns.

Interestingly enough, those who are advanced may find they need to change their program every 4 weeks. To be on the safe side, we will stick with 4 week program changes to keep adaptation working for us. Changes to your program can be as simple as changing the number of sets, reps, time you perform each exercise. Also, slight variations in exercises can be considered change. For example, changing from a pushup to an incline pushup will force the body to adapt.

Keep changing your program and include high-intensity exercise and your body will burn a lot of calories just trying to keep up. The harder you train, the better results you will get from EPOC. EPOC stands for Excess Post-Exercise Oxygen Consumption. EPOC is essentially the amount of calories you burn after your workout. EPOC is also called the Afterburn effect.

For fat loss, this is why it is better to train at 8 reps and lift a heavier weight than it is to perform 15 reps at a lighter weight. The intensity sparked by the higher weight will force the body to burn more calories to recover. In addition, the more muscle mass you maintain, the more energy your body will require to sustain itself.

So as you can see, weight training and high-intensity exercise burns more fat AFTER your workouts are over.

But don't take my word for it.

Please consider the following study revealed at the 2001 annual meeting of the American College of Sports Medicine:

Subjects currently training with weights underwent 2 individual weight workouts at different intensity levels. In session 1, they performed 2 sets of 15 repetitions (for 9 exercises) while in the other session they performed 2 sets of 8 repetitions (for 9 exercises). The results showed that the high intensity resistance training (2 sets of 8 repetitions) resulted in greater post-exercise energy expenditure.

Bottom Line: To burn more fat, we need to lift heavier weights. Weight training coupled with high intensity exercises is the best system to improve your body composition. We are hitting the body at both ends of the candle because these methods promote both energy expenditure and muscle growth!

I need you to forget the myth that slow, cardio is the most important aspect of a fat loss program.

Research disproves that trading time for calories is not the most effective way to lose fat. This may be an eye opener to you, but it is undeniable. Short high-intensity exercises coupled with weight training will yield superior results for fat loss.

Most of the trainers I know that train obese and overweight clients know that weight training and nutrition are far more important. In addition, when we turn on the 'Afterburners' with our short high-intensity exercises, fat doesn't stand a chance.

Dr. Angelo Tremblay at Laval University in Quebec conducted research that has shown that high-intensity interval training is more effective for fat loss than continuous low-intensity "aerobic" training. A 2006 study out of Australia showed similar results.

Bottom Line: Work harder, exercise shorter, and you'll bust through any fat loss plateaus you may be experiencing.

So why doesn't long, slow, boring cardio work?

The machines you use for cardio tell you how many calories you burn. Yes, you really are burning calories while performing long cardio sessions. Keep in mind most of these machines pad the numbers and tell you more than you are actually burning. Long and slow cardio doesn't deliver the 'Afterburn' because you have not placed any type of intensity on your body.

Think about walking from your front door to your car in the morning when you go to work. That's pretty easy, right? Once you sit down in your car, your body returns quickly to a normal rate.

What if you sprinted to your car and back to the front door, then back to your car? How long would it take for your body to recover?

That's right.. Afterburn. We create the afterburn with weight training and short high-intensity exercises.

I bet you have a lot of questions right now about how we put all of this together. That's fine because in the next chapter I've got tons of Q&A's that cover resistance training, cardio, and nutrition.

On to the workouts…

Chapter Two: What do you need to DO to build a golf body?

START HERE BEFORE BEGINNING PROGRAM.

Q: Which program should I start with?

Answer:

Those who are overweight and people who have not exercised in years will start with the Beginner workout program. If you have been exercising lightly and have only those last 10 to 20 pounds to lose, you will also start with the beginner program. If you do not have a solid base of fitness, you need to start with the beginner program to build a solid foundation.

People who regularly exercise should begin with the Intermediate program. To get the full benefit of Golf Specific training, you need to move in steps. The program is designed in a progressive manner and will strengthen areas that you may not have worked out before.

Every four weeks you will progress and change workouts. For example, you will perform the Beginner workout for 4 Weeks. At the end of the 4 weeks, begin the Intermediate workout. Perform the Intermediate workout for 4 weeks and then move to the advanced workout for 4 weeks.

At the end of the advanced workout, it is time to change yet again. We have other workout programs available that are golf related and challenging.

Q: But I am already exercising, where should I start? Should I really do the Intermediate workouts? I 'm afraid it will be too easy.

Answer:
Please start with the Intermediate Workout. Even if you perform CrossFit or other advanced workouts, I want you to begin with the Intermediate program. It will be challenging as long as you push yourself.

Q: So what's the "official" order of the Shed Pounds to Shave Strokes Workout program?

Answer:

Just to review...Beginners should start with Beginner Workouts while everyone else must start with the Intermediate Workout.

1. Beginner (4 Weeks)
2. Intermediate (4 Weeks)
3. Advanced (4 Weeks)

The Golf Specific workouts listed above will take you 3 months to complete. Once the above cycle is completed, you can start Shed Pounds to Shave Strokes all over again if you find you need to lose a few pounds. The important thing is to constantly be changing and keep your body guessing.

It is very important that you train within your limits with methods you are comfortable with. NEVER OVERDO THINGS!

1. ALWAYS practice an exercise with no weight or in a controlled environment before adding weight. If you are unsure how to perform a movement – ask us via Twitter, Facebook or Email!

2. If an exercise hurts or doesn't feel right – STOP. We can provide alternative movements or regressions to any exercise listed in the Shed Pounds to Shave Strokes manual. Simple ask us on for a substitution.

3. View your first week as 'practice' week. Use this time to learn the exercises with light weight. Perform one set of each exercise for the entire week. This will allow you to gauge how much weight you can handle and learn the movements well.

4. If you are feeling winded or rushed – take a break! There is no shame in needing a little extra rest between sets or exercises.

5. While our program does not use heavy weights, you may find times when you need a spotter. A spotter can help reduce risk of injury and add extra

motivation. Use a spotter if you are unsure if you can safely handle a weight you are lifting.

6. Regressive exercises may be needed if you are unable to perform some of the exercises listed in our program. In many cases, this will IMPROVE performance. Don't be afraid to use a regressive movement.

7. If you purchased any additional workouts for use with Shed Pounds to Shave Strokes, please complete the Shed Pounds to Shave Strokes workouts first. Once you have completed the system, you may begin the additional workouts.

8. Perform the Joint Mobility and Dynamic Warmups before EVERY workout. These are designed to increase your range of motion and decrease injury.

9. Do not start this program if you have an injury. Consult with your Physician on when you can begin.

10. Have fun!

The Workouts

The Beginner Workouts

Sedentary individuals and those who have not exercised consistently longer than 6-months need to start with the beginner workouts. That means if you have been sitting on a couch the past month, you need to start here.

Complete this series of workouts over the next 4 weeks. The workout has been designed to be done in the following order:

1.   Foam Rolling
2.   Warm Up
3.   Workout A
4.   Interval Training
5.   Stretching and Recovery

At the end of the routine, you can stretch any tight muscles.

Stretching & Recovery Guidelines

The cornerstone of adding distance AND consistency is to increase joint mobility and range of motion. Without an increased range of motion, you will NOT be as good as you can be. Simply, you will be 'limited'.

By limited, I mean you won't be able to fully hit each position for your golf swing. I don't care what swing you use, you won't be able to get in the proper slots if your mobility is limited.

To increase your range of motion, it is vital we perform certain movement's daily – even on off days. These movements do not take very long and will help the body to recover and thus add valuable yards to your game.

For most, the word recovery means to take a day off and rest. We do not adhere to this definition when speaking of joint mobility. Basically, if you don't use it, you WILL lose it. Being active actually helps our joints become more mobile.

Strategic Recovery performed on off days will prime your body for gains every single day.

TIP: Perform joint mobility and dynamic warm-ups each morning when you wake up if you are not working out. This ensures your body stays loose and pliable and gets you ready for the day.

On off days, perform the stretch and recovery program. Stretching and recovery is part of maintaining your body and increasing your range of motion. An increased range of motion will result in higher clubhead speed and the ability for more distance. In addition, the stretching and recovery exercises will help you get your body back in alignment and allow you a proper swing path.

Beginner Workout Guidelines

- ✓ Perform each Phase for 4 weeks and then transition to the next Phase of Shed Pounds to Shave Strokes. Morning workouts are recommended. If you are not currently following an exercise program or if you have a lot of weight to lose, you should start with the Beginner **Shed Pounds to Shave Strokes** program.

✓ The Beginner Workout should be followed for 4-6 weeks.

✓ After completing the Beginner Workout, you will be ready to move to the Advanced Workouts.

✓ If you are at an Intermediate Level of fitness, you can perform the Beginner Workouts for 2 weeks as a lead-in to the Advanced workouts.

✓ If there is a 3-digit number beside an exercise, it represents the lifting tempo.

– I.e. DB Reverse Lunge from Workout A in Phases 1 of the Advanced Program – The number is 2-0-1. Take 2 seconds to lower your body & without pausing, drive up to the start position in 1 second or less.

✓ Start every workout with the warm-up circuit and specific warm-up sets if required.

✓ Do not rest between exercises. Rest the recommended amount between circuits. You will find this rest time in the programs below.

✓ Finish each workout with stretching for the tight muscle groups only if desired.

✓ Please refer to the workout log sheets for more information.

✓ For a full description of how to perform any exercise in this workout, please see the Exercise Descriptions chapter.

Day 1 - Beginner Workout A

Equipment required: Bodyweight, Foam Roller, Yoga Mat

FOAM ROLLING (7-minutes)

- While this is optional, it is highly recommended you foam roll. Foam rolling is like getting a massage. It relaxes and prepares your deep tissue and muscles for work.

-

- Below is the bare minimum amount of time I recommend. Preferably, I would like you to spend as long as possible foam rolling.

1A) Hamstrings :30 secs / side

1B) Calves :30 secs / side

1C) Quads :30 secs / side

1D) IT Band :30 secs / side

1E) Hip Flexors :30 secs / side

1F) Low Back :30 secs / side

1G) Upper Back / Traps :30 secs / side

Warm-Up (5-Minutes)

- Go through the following with no rest between exercises. If you have a clock with a timer, you can use it to know when to switch to the next exercise.

2A) Torso Twists :60 seconds

2B) Side Bends :60 seconds

2C) Inchworms :60 seconds

2D) Superman Reaches :30 seconds

2E) Bodyweight Squats :60 seconds

2F) Straight Up Sit Up :30 seconds

Rest 1 minute and move on to the workout (3A).

Workout A (about 20-minutes)

Go through the following Superset with no rest between exercises.

3A) T Squat x 12 repetitions

3B) Stick-up x 12 repetitions

Rest 1 minute & repeat 1 more time for a total of 2 supersets.

Go through the following Superset with no rest between exercises.

4A) Single Leg Golf Posture Rotations x 8 repetitions per leg

4B) Pushup x 12 repetitions

Rest 1 minute & repeat 1 more time for a total of 2 supersets.

Go through the following Superset with no rest between exercises.

5A) Lying Hip Extension x 8 repetitions

5B) Plank on Elbows x 30 seconds hold

Rest 1 minute & repeat 1 more time for a total of 2 supersets.

Interval Workout A (about 20-minutes)

Perform the interval training directly after Workout A. This will ensure you get it done and can go about your regular activities without worrying about coming back to this.

- ✓ Choose from the following: Treadmill, Bicycle, Elliptical, Hills, Track, Stairs
- ✓ Warm-up for 4 minutes getting progressively more intense with time.
- ✓ Perform an interval by exercising for 30 seconds at a "harder than normal cardio" pace (at a 7/10 level of effort).
- ✓ Follow that with "active rest" for 90 seconds by exercising at a slow pace (at a subjective 3/10 level of effort).
- ✓ Repeat for a total of 6 intervals.

- ✓ Finish with 5 minutes of very low intensity (3/10) exercise for a cool-down.
- ✓ This workout takes approximately 20 minutes.

GOLF Fitness:
Shed Pounds to Shave Strokes

	Workout A / Beginner	
Foam Rolling (7-Minutes)	Side 1	Side 2
1A) Hamstrings :30 secs / side		
1B) Calves :30 secs / side		
1C) Quads :30 secs / side		
1D) IT Band :30 secs / side		
1E) Hip Flexors :30 secs / side		
1F) Low Back :30 secs / side		
1G) Upper Back :30 secs / side		
Warm-Up (5-Minutes)	Set 1	
2A) Torso Twists :60 seconds		
2B) Side Bends :60 seconds		
2C) Inchworms :60 seconds		
2D) Superman Reaches :30 seconds		
2E) Bodyweight Squats :60 seconds		
2F) Straight Up Sit up :30 seconds		
Workout A (about 20-minutes)	Set 1	Set 2
3A) T Squat x 12		
3B) Stick-up x 12		
4A) Single Leg Golf Posture Rotations x 8 each leg		
4B) Pushup x 12		
5A) Lying Hip Extension x 8		
5B) Plank on Elbows x 30 Seconds		

Interval Program A (about 20-minutes)	Time	Type	Intensity
Warm Up	3 Min	Warm	3 of 10
Warm Up	1 Min	Warm	5 of 10
Interval 1	30 Sec	Hard	7 of 10
Rest Interval	90 sec	Easy	3 of 10
Interval 2	30 Sec	Hard	7 of 10
Rest Interval	90 sec	Easy	3 of 10
Interval 3	30 Sec	Hard	7 of 10
Rest Interval	90 sec	Easy	3 of 10
Interval 4	30 Sec	Hard	7 of 10
Rest Interval	90 sec	Easy	3 of 10
Interval 5	30 Sec	Hard	7 of 10
Rest Interval	90 sec	Easy	3 of 10
Interval 6	30 Sec	Hard	7 of 10
Cool Down	5 Min	Cool	3 of 10

Day 2 - Stretch & Recovery Day

Equipment required: Bodyweight, Yoga Mat

GOLF Fitness:
Shed Pounds to **Shave Strokes**

	Stretch and Recovery
Mobility	Set 1
1) Three Plane Neck :30 seconds	
2) Shoulder Circles :30 seconds	
3) Fist Exercise :30 seconds	
4) Wrist Rotations :30 seconds	
5) Elbow Circles :30 seconds	
6) Egyptian :30 seconds	
7) Arm Circles :30 seconds	
8) Hula Hoop :30 seconds	
9) Ankle Circles :30 seconds	
10) Knee Circles :30 seconds	
Flexibility	Set 1
1) Toe Hang :30 seconds	
2) Cobra :30 seconds	
3) Spine Rotation w/ Club :30 seconds	
4) Head Turner :30 seconds (each side)	
5) Headache Buster :30 seconds (each side)	
6) Chest Stretch 1 :30 seconds (each side)	
7) Chest Stretch 2 :30 seconds (each side)	
8) Backswing Angel :30 seconds	
9) Wrist Flexion :30 seconds (each side)	
10) Shoulder Stretch :30 seconds (each side)	
11) Kneeling Hip Flexor :30 seconds (each side)	
12) Piriformis :30 seconds (each side)	
13) Seated Groin Stretch :30 seconds (each side)	
14) Calf Stretch :30 seconds (each side)	
Interval Program (Rest Day)	
Light activity (golf) or rest.	

Day 3 - Beginner Workout B

Equipment required: Bodyweight, Foam Roller, Yoga Mat

FOAM ROLLING (7-minutes)

While this is optional, it is highly recommended you foam roll. Foam rolling is like getting a massage. It relaxes and prepares your deep tissue and muscles for work. Below is the bare minimum amount of time I recommend. Preferably, I would like you to spend as long as possible foam rolling.

1A) Hamstrings :30 secs / side

1B) Calves :30 secs / side

1C) Quads :30 secs / side

1D) IT Band :30 secs / side

1E) Hip Flexors :30 secs / side

1F) Low Back :30 secs / side

1G) Upper Back / Traps :30 secs / side

Warm-Up (5-Minutes)

Go through the following with no rest between exercises. If you have a clock with a timer, you can use it to know when to switch to the next exercise.

2A) Torso Twists :60 seconds

2B) Side Bends :60 seconds

2C) Inchworms :60 seconds

2D) Superman Reaches :30 seconds

2E) Bodyweight Squats :60 seconds

2F) Straight Up Sit Up :30 seconds

Rest 1 minute and move on to the workout (3A).

Workout B (about 20-minutes)

Go through the following Superset with no rest between exercises.

3A) Y Squat x 12 repetitions.

3B) Cross Crawl x 12 repetitions per side.

Rest 1 minute & repeat 1 more time for a total of 2 supersets.

Go through the following Superset with no rest between exercises.

4A) Single Leg Cone Reach x 8 repetitions per side.

4B) Incline Pushups x 12 repetitions.

Rest 1 minute & repeat 1 more time for a total of 2 supersets.

Go through the following Superset with no rest between exercises.

5A) Floor Cobra x 8 repetitions.

5B) Side Plank x 30 seconds hold each side.

Rest 1 minute & repeat 1 more time for a total of 2 supersets.

Interval Workout B (about 20-minutes)

Perform the interval training directly after Workout A. This will ensure you get it done and can go about your regular activities without worrying about coming back to this.

- ✓ Choose from the following: Treadmill, Bicycle, Elliptical, Hills, Track, Stairs
- ✓ Warm-up for 4 minutes getting progressively more intense with time.
- ✓ Perform an interval by exercising for 30 seconds at a "harder than normal cardio" pace (at a 7/10 level of effort).
- ✓ Follow that with "active rest" for 90 seconds by exercising at a slow pace (at a subjective 3/10 level of effort).
- ✓ Repeat for a total of 6 intervals.
- ✓ Finish with 5 minutes of very low intensity (3/10) exercise for a cool-down.
- ✓ This workout takes approximately 20 minutes.

GOLF Fitness:
Shed Pounds to Shave Strokes

	Workout B / Beginner	
Foam Rolling (7-Minutes)	Side 1	Side 2
1A) Hamstrings :30 secs / side		
1B) Calves :30 secs / side		
1C) Quads :30 secs / side		
1D) IT Band :30 secs / side		
1E) Hip Flexors :30 secs / side		
1F) Low Back :30 secs / side		
1G) Upper Back :30 secs / side		
Warm-Up (5-Minutes)	Set 1	
2A) Torso Twists :60 seconds		
2B) Side Bends :60 seconds		
2C) Inchworms :60 seconds		
2D) Superman Reaches :30 seconds		
2E) Bodyweight Squats :60 seconds		
2F) Straight Up Sit up :30 seconds		
Workout B (about 20-minutes)	Set 1	Set 2
3A) Y Squat x 12		
3B) Cross Crawl x 12		
4A) Single Leg Cone Reach x 8 each side		
4B) Incline Pushups x 12		
5A) Floor Cobra x 8		
5B) Side Plank x 30 seconds hold each side		

Interval Program B (about 20-minutes)	Time	Type	Intensity
Warm Up	3 Min	Warm	3 of 10
Warm Up	1 Min	Warm	5 of 10
Interval 1	30 Sec	Hard	7 of 10
Rest Interval	90 sec	Easy	3 of 10
Interval 2	30 Sec	Hard	7 of 10
Rest Interval	90 Sec	Easy	3 of 10
Interval 3	30 Sec	Hard	7 of 10
Rest Interval	90 sec	Easy	3 of 10
Interval 4	30 Sec	Hard	7 of 10
Rest Interval	90 sec	Easy	3 of 10
Interval 5	30 Sec	Hard	8 of 10
Rest Interval	90 sec	Easy	3 of 10
Interval 6	30 Sec	Hard	7 of 10
Cool Down	5 Min	Cool	3 of 10

Day 4 - Stretch & Recovery Day

Equipment required: Bodyweight, Yoga Mat

GOLF Fitness:
Shed Pounds to Shave Strokes

	Stretch and Recovery
Mobility	Set 1
1) Three Plane Neck :30 seconds	
2) Shoulder Circles :30 seconds	
3) Fist Exercise :30 seconds	
4) Wrist Rotations :30 seconds	
5) Elbow Circles :30 seconds	
6) Egyptian :30 seconds	
7) Arm Circles :30 seconds	
8) Hula Hoop :30 seconds	
9) Ankle Circles :30 seconds	
10) Knee Circles :30 seconds	
Flexibility	Set 1
1) Toe Hang :30 seconds	
2) Cobra :30 seconds	
3) Spine Rotation w/ Club :30 seconds	
4) Head Turner :30 seconds (each side)	
5) Headache Buster :30 seconds (each side)	
6) Chest Stretch 1 :30 seconds (each side)	
7) Chest Stretch 2 :30 seconds (each side)	
8) Backswing Angel :30 seconds	
9) Wrist Flexion :30 seconds (each side)	
10) Shoulder Stretch :30 seconds (each side)	
11) Kneeling Hip Flexor :30 seconds (each side)	
12) Piriformis :30 seconds (each side)	
13) Seated Groin Stretch :30 seconds (each side)	
14) Calf Stretch :30 seconds (each side)	
Interval Program (Rest Day)	
Light activity (golf) or rest.	

Day 5 - Beginner Workout C

Equipment required: Bodyweight, Foam Roller, Yoga Mat

FOAM ROLLING (7-minutes)

While this is optional, it is highly recommended you foam roll. Foam rolling is like getting a massage. It relaxes and prepares your deep tissue and muscles for work. Below is the bare minimum amount of time I recommend. Preferably, I would like you to spend as long as possible foam rolling.

1A) Hamstrings :30 secs / side

1B) Calves :30 secs / side

1C) Quads :30 secs / side

1D) IT Band :30 secs / side

1E) Hip Flexors :30 secs / side

1F) Low Back :30 secs / side

1G) Upper Back / Traps :30 secs / side

Warm-Up (5-Minutes)

Go through the following with no rest between exercises. If you have a clock with a timer, you can use it to know when to switch to the next exercise.

2A) Torso Twists :60 seconds

2B) Side Bends :60 seconds

2C) Inchworms :60 seconds

2D) Superman Reaches :30 seconds

2E) Bodyweight Squats :60 seconds

2F) Straight Up Sit Up :30 seconds

Rest 1 minute and move on to the workout (3A).

Workout C (about 16-minutes)

3A) Prisoner Squat x 12 repetitions.

3B) Kneeling or Regular Pushup x 15 repetitions.

3C) Plank x 30 second hold.

3D) 1-Leg Hip Extension x 8 repetitions per side.

3E) Side Plank x 30 second hold per side.

3F) Wall Squat x 30 Second hold.

3G) Horse Reach x 8 repetitions each side

3H) Stick-up x 10 repetitions.

Rest 1 minute & repeat 2 more times for a total of 3 supersets.

GOLF Fitness:
Shed Pounds to Shave Strokes

Foam Rolling (7-Minutes)	Workout C / Beginner	
	Side 1	Side 2
1A) Hamstrings :30 secs / side		
1B) Calves :30 secs / side		
1C) Quads :30 secs / side		
1D) IT Band :30 secs / side		
1E) Hip Flexors :30 secs / side		
1F) Low Back :30 secs / side		
1G) Upper Back :30 secs / side		
Warm-Up (5-Minutes)	Set 1	
2A) Torso Twists :60 seconds		
2B) Side Bends :60 seconds		
2C) Inchworms :60 seconds		
2D) Superman Reaches :30 seconds		
2E) Bodyweight Squats :60 seconds		
2F) Straight Up Sit up :30 seconds		
Workout C (about 20-minutes)	Set 1	Set 2
3A) Prisoner Squat x 12		
3B) Kneeling or Regular Pushup x 15		
3C) Plank x 30 second hold		
3D) 1-Leg Hip Extension x 8 each leg		
3E) Side Plank x 30 second hold		
3F) Wall Squat x 30 Second hold		
3G) Horse Reach x 8 each side		
3H) Stick-up x 10		
Interval Program (Rest Day)		

Play 9 Holes or Driving Range and Short Game practice.
Aim for two hours of practice or play.
If you play and are capable of walking the course, lighten your
bag so that you have the bare essentials.

If weather is not acceptable for golf, walking on a treadmill
will work fine.

Days 6 & 7 - Off Days

Equipment required: Golf Clubs, Treadmill, Bicycle, Mall

Most of us lead sedentary lifestyles. As golfers though, we have an off day activity we can plug in for at least 30 minutes of easy activity. Putting on the practice green, going to the driving range, walking nine holes all qualify as easy activity. Even riding in a cart and playing golf count as easy activity.

If you find you can't play golf due to cold weather or rain you may walk on a treadmill. Go to the mall and walk around. The key is getting off your butt and doing something. Stop watching the TV and move around.

Yoga and Pilates are good off day activities as well. Just don't overdo them, our workouts are going to be strenuous during the week.

The more overweight you are, the more you should focus on non-weight bearing activities. Swimming and bicycling are great activities.

Remember, it's an easy activity, it should NOT be intense.

The Intermediate Workouts

Sedentary individuals and those who have not exercised consistently longer than 6-months need to start with the beginner workouts. That means if you have been sitting on a couch the past month, you need to start here.

It is highly recommended that you only start here if you would consider yourself advanced in terms of fitness. All others should start with the beginner program.

Complete this series of workouts over the next 4 weeks.

The workout has been designed to be done in the following order:

1. Foam Rolling
2. Warm Up
3. Workout A
4. Interval Training

At the end of the routine, you can stretch any tight muscles.

On off days, perform the stretch and recovery program. Stretching and recovery is part of maintaining your body and increasing your range of motion. An increased range of motion will result in higher clubhead speed and the ability for more distance. In addition, the stretching and recovery exercises will help you get your body back in alignment and allow you a proper swing path.

Intermediate Workout Guidelines

✓ Perform each Phase for 4 weeks and then transition to the next Phase of Shed Pounds to Shave Strokes. Morning workouts are recommended. If you are not currently following an exercise program or if you have a lot of weight to lose, you should start with the Beginner **Shed Pounds to Shave Strokes** program.

✓ The Beginner Workout should be followed for 4-6 weeks.

✓ After completing the Beginner Workout, you will be ready to move to the Advanced Workouts.

✓ If you are at an Intermediate Level of fitness, you can perform the Beginner Workouts for 2 weeks as a lead-in to the Advanced workouts.

✓ If there is a 3-digit number beside an exercise, it represents the lifting tempo.

– I.e. DB Reverse Lunge from Workout A in Phases 1 of the Advanced Program – The number is 2-0-1. Take 2 seconds to lower your body & without pausing, drive up to the start position in 1 second or less.

✓ Start every workout with the warm-up circuit and specific warm-up sets if required.

✓ Do not rest between exercises. Rest the recommended amount between circuits. You will find this rest time in the programs below.

✓ Finish each workout with stretching for the tight muscle groups only if desired.

✓ Please refer to the workout log sheets for more information.

✓ For a full description of how to perform any exercise in this workout, please see the Exercise Descriptions chapter.

Day 1 - Intermediate Workout A

Equipment required: Bodyweight, Foam Roller, Yoga Mat

FOAM ROLLING (7-minutes)

While this is optional, it is highly recommended you foam roll. Foam rolling is like getting a massage. It relaxes and prepares your deep tissue and muscles for work. Below is the bare minimum amount of time I recommend. Preferably, I would like you to spend as long as possible foam rolling.

1A) Hamstrings :30 secs / side

1B) Calves :30 secs / side

1C) Quads :30 secs / side

1D) IT Band :30 secs / side

1E) Hip Flexors :30 secs / side

1F) Low Back :30 secs / side

1G) Upper Back / Traps :30 secs / side

Warm-Up (5-Minutes)

Go through the following with no rest between exercises. If you have a clock with a timer, you can use it to know when to switch to the next exercise.

2A) Torso Twists :60 seconds

2B) Side Bends :60 seconds

2C) Inchworms :60 seconds

2D) Superman Reaches :30 seconds

2E) Bodyweight Squats :60 seconds

2F) Straight Up Sit Up :30 seconds

Rest 1 minute and move on to the workout (3A).

Workout A (about 20-minutes)

Go through the following Superset with no rest between exercises.

3A) DB Bench Press x 12 repetitions.

3B) DB Bench Row x 12 repetitions per side.

Rest 1 minute & repeat 2 more times for a total of 3 supersets.

Go through the following Superset with no rest between exercises.
4A) DB Squat x 12 repetitions.
4B) Single-Leg Dumbbell Curl x 8 repetitions per side.
Rest 1 minute & repeat 2 more times for a total of 3 supersets.

Go through the following Superset with no rest between exercises.
5A) Stability Ball Leg Curl x 8 repetitions.
5B) Plank on Elbows x 45 seconds hold.
Rest 1 minute & repeat 2 more times for a total of 3 supersets.

Interval Workout A (about 20-minutes)
Perform the interval training directly after Workout A. This will ensure you get it done and can go about your regular activities without worrying about coming back to this.
- ✓ Choose from the following: Treadmill, Bicycle, Elliptical, Hills, Track, Stairs
- ✓ Warm-up for 4 minutes getting progressively more intense with time.

✓ Perform an interval by exercising for 30 seconds at a "harder than normal cardio" pace (at a 7/10 level of effort).

✓ Follow that with "active rest" for 90 seconds by exercising at a slow pace (at a subjective 3/10 level of effort).

✓ Repeat for a total of 6 intervals.

✓ Finish with 5 minutes of very low intensity (3/10) exercise for a cool-down.

✓ This workout takes approximately 20 minutes.

GOLF Fitness:
Shed Pounds to Shave Strokes

	Workout A / Intermediate		
Foam Rolling (7-Minutes)	Side 1	Side 2	
1A) Hamstrings :30 secs / side			
1B) Calves :30 secs / side			
1C) Quads :30 secs / side			
1D) IT Band :30 secs / side			
1E) Hip Flexors :30 secs / side			
1F) Low Back :30 secs / side			
1G) Upper Back :30 secs / side			
Warm-Up (5-Minutes)	Set 1		
2A) Torso Twists :60 seconds			
2B) Side Bends :60 seconds			
2C) Inchworms :60 seconds			
2D) Superman Reaches :30 seconds			
2E) Bodyweight Squats :60 seconds			
2F) Straight Up Sit up :30 seconds			
Workout A (about 20-minutes)	Set 1	Set 2	Set 3
3A) DB Bench Press x 12			
3B) DB Bench Row x 12			
4A) DB Squat x 12			
4B) Single-Leg Dumbbell Curl x 8 each side			
5A) Stability Ball Leg Curl x 8			
5B) Plank on Elbows x 45 seconds			
Interval Program A (about 20-minutes)	Time	Type	Intensity
Warm Up	3 Min	Warm	3 of 10
Warm Up	1 Min	Warm	5 of 10
Interval 1	30 Sec	Hard	7 of 10
Rest Interval	90 sec	Easy	3 of 10
Interval 2	30 Sec	Hard	7 of 10
Rest Interval	90 Sec	Easy	3 of 10
Interval 3	30 Sec	Hard	7 of 10
Rest Interval	90 sec	Easy	3 of 10
Interval 4	30 Sec	Hard	7 of 10
Rest Interval	90 sec	Easy	3 of 10
Interval 5	30 Sec	Hard	7 of 10
Rest Interval	90 sec	Easy	3 of 10
Interval 6	30 Sec	Hard	7 of 10
Cool Down	5 Min	Cool	3 of 10

Day 2 - Stretch & Recovery Day

Equipment required: Bodyweight, Yoga Mat

GOLF Fitness:
Shed Pounds to **Shave Strokes**

	Stretch and Recovery
Mobility	Set 1
1) Three Plane Neck :30 seconds	
2) Shoulder Circles :30 seconds	
3) Fist Exercise :30 seconds	
4) Wrist Rotations :30 seconds	
5) Elbow Circles :30 seconds	
6) Egyptian :30 seconds	
7) Arm Circles :30 seconds	
8) Hula Hoop :30 seconds	
9) Ankle Circles :30 seconds	
10) Knee Circles :30 seconds	
Flexibility	Set 1
1) Toe Hang :30 seconds	
2) Cobra :30 seconds	
3) Spine Rotation w/ Club :30 seconds	
4) Head Turner :30 seconds (each side)	
5) Headache Buster :30 seconds (each side)	
6) Chest Stretch 1 :30 seconds (each side)	
7) Chest Stretch 2 :30 seconds (each side)	
8) Backswing Angel :30 seconds	
9) Wrist Flexion :30 seconds (each side)	
10) Shoulder Stretch :30 seconds (each side)	
11) Kneeling Hip Flexor :30 seconds (each side)	
12) Piriformis :30 seconds (each side)	
13) Seated Groin Stretch :30 seconds (each side)	
14) Calf Stretch :30 seconds (each side)	
Interval Program (Rest Day)	
Light activity (golf) or rest.	

Day 3 - Intermediate Workout B

Equipment required: Bodyweight, Foam Roller, Yoga Mat

FOAM ROLLING (7-minutes)

While this is optional, it is highly recommended you foam roll. Foam rolling is like getting a massage. It relaxes and prepares your deep tissue and muscles for work. Below is the bare minimum amount of time I recommend. Preferably, I would like you to spend as long as possible foam rolling.

1A) Hamstrings :30 secs / side

1B) Calves :30 secs / side

1C) Quads :30 secs / side

1D) IT Band :30 secs / side

1E) Hip Flexors :30 secs / side

1F) Low Back :30 secs / side

1G) Upper Back / Traps :30 secs / side

Warm-Up (5-Minutes)

Go through the following with no rest between exercises. If you have a clock with a timer, you can use it to know when to switch to the next exercise.

2A) Torso Twists :60 seconds

2B) Side Bends :60 seconds

2C) Inchworms :60 seconds

2D) Superman Reaches :30 seconds

2E) Bodyweight Squats :60 seconds

2F) Straight Up Sit Up :30 seconds

Rest 1 minute and move on to the workout (3A).

Workout B (about 20-minutes)

Go through the following Superset with no rest between exercises.

3A) DB Step-Up to Balance x 8 repetitions per side.

3B) DB Woodchop x 8 repetitions per side.

Rest 1 minute & repeat 2 more times for a total of 3 supersets.

Go through the following Superset with no rest between exercises.

4A) Walkout Pushups x 15 repetitions.

4B) Cross Crawl x 15 repetitions.

Rest 1 minute & repeat 2 more times for a total of 3 supersets.

Go through the following Superset with no rest between exercises.

5A) Floor Cobra x 15 repetitions.

5B) Side Plank x 45 seconds hold per side.

Rest 1 minute & repeat 2 more times for a total of 3 supersets.

Interval Workout B (about 20-minutes)

Perform the interval training directly after Workout A. This will ensure you get it done and can go about your regular activities without worrying about coming back to this.

✓ Choose from the following: Treadmill, Bicycle, Elliptical, Hills, Track, Stairs

✓ Warm-up for 4 minutes getting progressively more intense with time.

✓ Perform an interval by exercising for 30 seconds at a "harder than normal cardio" pace (at a 8/10 level of effort).

✓ Follow that with "active rest" for 90 seconds by exercising at a slow pace (at a subjective 3/10 level of effort).

✓ Repeat for a total of 6 intervals.

✓ Finish with 5 minutes of very low intensity (3/10) exercise for a cool-down.

✓ This workout takes approximately 20 minutes.

GOLF Fitness:
Shed Pounds to **Shave Strokes**

Foam Rolling (7-Minutes)	Workout B / Intermediate	
	Side 1	Side 2
1A) Hamstrings :30 secs / side		
1B) Calves :30 secs / side		
1C) Quads :30 secs / side		
1D) IT Band :30 secs / side		
1E) Hip Flexors :30 secs / side		
1F) Low Back :30 secs / side		
1G) Upper Back :30 secs / side		

Warm-Up (5-Minutes)	Set 1
2A) Torso Twists :60 seconds	
2B) Side Bends :60 seconds	
2C) Inchworms :60 seconds	
2D) Superman Reaches :30 seconds	
2E) Bodyweight Squats :60 seconds	
2F) Straight Up Sit up :30 seconds	

Workout B (about 20-minutes)	Set 1	Set 2	Set 3
3A) DB Step-Up to Balance x 8 each side			
3B) DB Woodchop x 8 each side			
4A) Walkout Pushups x 15			
4B) Cross Crawl x 15			
5A) Floor Cobra x 15			
5B) Side Plank x 45 seconds			

Interval Program B (about 20-minutes)	Time	Type	Intensity
Warm Up	3 Min	Warm	3 of 10
Warm Up	1 Min	Warm	5 of 10
Interval 1	30 Sec	Hard	8 of 10
Rest Interval	90 sec	Easy	3 of 10
Interval 2	30 Sec	Hard	8 of 10
Rest Interval	90 Sec	Easy	3 of 10
Interval 3	30 Sec	Hard	8 of 10
Rest Interval	90 sec	Easy	3 of 10
Interval 4	30 Sec	Hard	8 of 10
Rest Interval	90 sec	Easy	3 of 10
Interval 5	30 Sec	Hard	8 of 10
Rest Interval	90 sec	Easy	3 of 10
Interval 6	30 Sec	Hard	8 of 10
Cool Down	5 Min	Cool	3 of 10

Day 4 - Stretch & Recovery Day

Equipment required: Bodyweight, Yoga Mat

GOLF Fitness:
Shed Pounds to **Shave Strokes**

	Stretch and Recovery
Mobility	Set 1
1) Three Plane Neck :30 seconds	
2) Shoulder Circles :30 seconds	
3) Fist Exercise :30 seconds	
4) Wrist Rotations :30 seconds	
5) Elbow Circles :30 seconds	
6) Egyptian :30 seconds	
7) Arm Circles :30 seconds	
8) Hula Hoop :30 seconds	
9) Ankle Circles :30 seconds	
10) Knee Circles :30 seconds	
Flexibility	Set 1
1) Toe Hang :30 seconds	
2) Cobra :30 seconds	
3) Spine Rotation w/ Club :30 seconds	
4) Head Turner :30 seconds (each side)	
5) Headache Buster :30 seconds (each side)	
6) Chest Stretch 1 :30 seconds (each side)	
7) Chest Stretch 2 :30 seconds (each side)	
8) Backswing Angel :30 seconds	
9) Wrist Flexion :30 seconds (each side)	
10) Shoulder Stretch :30 seconds (each side)	
11) Kneeling Hip Flexor :30 seconds (each side)	
12) Piriformis :30 seconds (each side)	
13) Seated Groin Stretch :30 seconds (each side)	
14) Calf Stretch :30 seconds (each side)	
Interval Program (Rest Day)	
Light activity (golf) or rest.	

Day 5 - Intermediate Workout C

Equipment required: Bodyweight, Foam Roller, Yoga Mat

FOAM ROLLING (7-minutes)

While this is optional, it is highly recommended you foam roll. Foam rolling is like getting a massage. It relaxes and prepares your deep tissue and muscles for work. Below is the bare minimum amount of time I recommend. Preferably, I would like you to spend as long as possible foam rolling.

1A) Hamstrings :30 secs / side

1B) Calves :30 secs / side

1C) Quads :30 secs / side

1D) IT Band :30 secs / side

1E) Hip Flexors :30 secs / side

1F) Low Back :30 secs / side

1G) Upper Back / Traps :30 secs / side

Warm-Up (5-Minutes)

Go through the following with no rest between exercises. If you have a clock with a timer, you can use it to know when to switch to the next exercise.

2A) Torso Twists :60 seconds

2B) Side Bends :60 seconds

2C) Inchworms :60 seconds

2D) Superman Reaches :30 seconds

2E) Bodyweight Squats :60 seconds

2F) Straight Up Sit Up :30 seconds

Rest 1 minute and move on to the workout (3A).

Workout C (about 16-minutes)

3A) Prisoner Squat x 20 repetitions.

3B) Decline Pushup (feet on ball) x 15 repetitions.

3C) Side Plank x 30 second hold.

3D) Stability Ball Hip Extension x 8 repetitions.

3E) Ball Cobra (no weights) x 30 second hold.

3F) Wall Squat x 45 second hold.

3G) Horse Reach x 12 repetitions per side.

3H) Squat Thrust (no pushup) x 8 repetitions.

Rest 1 minute & repeat 2 more times for a total of 3 supersets.

GOLF Fitness:
Shed Pounds to **Shave Strokes**

	Workout C / Intermediate		
Foam Rolling (7-Minutes)	Side 1	Side 2	
1A) Hamstrings :30 secs / side			
1B) Calves :30 secs / side			
1C) Quads :30 secs / side			
1D) IT Band :30 secs / side			
1E) Hip Flexors :30 secs / side			
1F) Low Back :30 secs / side			
1G) Upper Back :30 secs / side			
Warm-Up (5-Minutes)	Set 1		
2A) Torso Twists :60 seconds			
2B) Side Bends :60 seconds			
2C) Inchworms :60 seconds			
2D) Superman Reaches :30 seconds			
2E) Bodyweight Squats :60 seconds			
2F) Straight Up Sit up :30 seconds			
Workout C (about 20-minutes)	Set 1	Set 2	Set 3
3A) Prisoner Squat x 20			
3B) Decline Pushup (feet on ball) x 15			
3C) Side Plank x 30 second hold			
3D) Stability Ball Hip Extension x 8 each leg			
3E) Ball Cobra (no weights) x 30 second hold			
3F) Wall Squat x 45 Second hold			
3G) Horse Reach x 12 each side			
3H) Squat Thrust (no pushup) x 8			

Interval Program (Rest Day)

Play 9 Holes or Driving Range and Short Game practice.
Aim for two hours of practice or play.
If you play and are capable of walking the course, lighten your
bag so that you have the bare essentials.

If weather is not acceptable for golf, walking on a treadmill
will work fine.

Days 6 & 7 - Off Days

Equipment required: Golf Clubs, Treadmill, Bicycle, Mall

Most of us lead sedentary lifestyles. As golfers though, we have an off day activity we can plug in for at least 30 minutes of easy activity. Putting on the practice green, going to the driving range, walking nine holes all qualify as easy activity. Even riding in a cart and playing golf count as easy activity.

If you find you can't play golf due to cold weather or rain you may walk on a treadmill. Go to the mall and walk around. The key is getting off your butt and doing something. Stop watching the TV and move around.

Yoga and Pilates are good off day activities as well. Just don't overdo them, our workouts are going to be strenuous during the week.

The more overweight you are, the more you should focus on non-weight bearing activities. Swimming and bicycling are great activities.

Remember, it's an easy activity, it should NOT be intense.

The Advanced Workouts

Congrats! You've made it to the final workout. This is where the rubber meets the road in terms of golf performance. Additional dynamic power moves are now added to the routine. This provides the spark that ignites higher club head speed.

Only attempt this workout if you have successfully completed the Intermediate workouts! While you may feel ready, it is important to do the program in the order it was designed.

Complete this series of workouts over the next 4 weeks.

The advanced workout has been designed to be done in the following order:

1.   Foam Rolling
2.   Warm Up
3.   Workout A
4.   Interval Training

At the end of the routine, you can stretch any tight muscles.

On off days, perform the stretch and recovery program. Stretching and recovery is part of maintaining your body and increasing your range of motion. An increased range of motion will result in higher clubhead speed and the ability for more distance. In addition, the stretching and recovery exercises will help you get your body back in alignment and allow you a proper swing path.

Advanced Workout Guidelines

✓ Perform each Phase for 4 weeks and then transition to the next Phase of Shed Pounds to Shave Strokes. Morning workouts are recommended. If you are not currently following an exercise program or if you have a lot of weight to lose, you should start with the Beginner **Shed Pounds to Shave Strokes** program.

✓ The Beginner Workout should be followed for 4-6 weeks.

✓ After completing the Beginner Workout, you will be ready to move to the Advanced Workouts.

✓ If you are at an Intermediate Level of fitness, you can perform the Beginner Workouts for 2 weeks as a lead-in to the Advanced workouts.

✓ If there is a 3-digit number beside an exercise, it represents the lifting tempo.

– I.e. DB Reverse Lunge from Workout A in Phases

1 of the Advanced Program – The number is 2-0-1. Take 2 seconds to lower your body & without pausing, drive up to the start position in 1 second or less.

✓ Start every workout with the warm-up circuit and specific warm-up sets if required.

✓ Do not rest between exercises. Rest the recommended amount between circuits. You will find this rest time in the programs below.

✓ Finish each workout with stretching for the tight muscle groups only if desired.

✓ Please refer to the workout log sheets for more information.

✓ For a full description of how to perform any exercise in this workout, please see the Exercise Descriptions chapter.

Day 1 - Advanced Workout A

Equipment required: Dumbbells, Stability Ball, Bench, Medicine Ball

FOAM ROLLING (7-minutes)

While this is optional, it is highly recommended you foam roll. Foam rolling is like getting a massage. It relaxes and prepares your deep tissue and muscles for work. Below is the bare minimum amount of time I recommend. Preferably, I would like you to spend as long as possible foam rolling.

1A) Hamstrings :30 secs / side

1B) Calves :30 secs / side

1C) Quads :30 secs / side

1D) IT Band :30 secs / side

1E) Hip Flexors :30 secs / side

1F) Low Back :30 secs / side

1G) Upper Back / Traps :30 secs / side

Warm-Up (5-Minutes)

Go through the following with no rest between exercises. If you have a clock with a timer, you can use it to know when to switch to the next exercise.

2A) Torso Twists :60 seconds

2B) Side Bends :60 seconds

2C) Inchworms :60 seconds

2D) Superman Reaches :30 seconds

2E) Bodyweight Squats :60 seconds

2F) Straight Up Sit Up :30 seconds

Rest 1 minute and move on to the workout (3A).

Workout A (about 20-minutes)

Go through the following Superset with no rest between exercises.

3A) Single-Leg Dumbbell Squat x 8 repetitions per side.

3B) DB Warrior Row x 12 repetitions per side.

Rest 1 minute & repeat 2 more times for a total of 3 supersets.

Go through the following Superset with no rest between exercises.

4A) DB Stability Ball Press x 12 repetitions.

4B) DB Squat, Curl, Press x 12 repetitions.

Rest 1 minute & repeat 2 more times for a total of 3 supersets.

Go through the following Superset with no rest between exercises.

5A) Prone Twister With Stability Ball x 8 repetitions per side.

5B) Medicine Ball Slam x 12 repetitions.

Rest 1 minute & repeat 2 more times for a total of 3 supersets.

Interval Workout A (about 20-minutes)

Perform the interval training directly after Workout A. This will ensure you get it done and can go about your regular activities without worrying about coming back to this.

✓ Choose from the following: Treadmill, Bicycle, Elliptical, Hills, Track, Stairs

✓ Warm-up for 4 minutes getting progressively more intense with time.

✓ Perform an interval by exercising for 30 seconds at a "harder than normal cardio" pace (at a 9/10 level of effort).

✓ Follow that with "active rest" for 90 seconds by exercising at a slow pace (at a subjective 3/10 level of effort).

✓ Repeat for a total of 6 intervals.

✓ Finish with 5 minutes of very low intensity (3/10) exercise for a cool-down.

✓ This workout takes approximately 20 minutes.

GOLF Fitness:
Shed Pounds to Shave Strokes

	Workout A / Advanced	
Foam Rolling (7-Minutes)	Side 1	Side 2
1A) Hamstrings :30 secs / side		
1B) Calves :30 secs / side		
1C) Quads :30 secs / side		
1D) IT Band :30 secs / side		
1E) Hip Flexors :30 secs / side		
1F) Low Back :30 secs / side		
1G) Upper Back :30 secs / side		

	Set 1		
Warm-Up (5-Minutes)			
2A) Torso Twists :60 seconds			
2B) Side Bends :60 seconds			
2C) Inchworms :60 seconds			
2D) Superman Reaches :30 seconds			
2E) Bodyweight Squats :60 seconds			
2F) Straight Up Sit up :30 seconds			

Workout A (about 20-minutes)	Set 1	Set 2	Set 3
3A) Single-Leg Dumbbell Squat x 8 each side			
3B) DB Warrior Row x 12			
4A) DB Stability Ball Press x 12			
4B) DB Squat, Curl, Press x 12			
5A) Prone Twister With Stability Ball x 8 per side			
5B) Medicine Ball Slam x 12			

Interval Program A (about 20-minutes)	Time	Type	Intensity
Warm Up	3 Min	Warm	4 of 10
Warm Up	1 Min	Warm	5 of 10
Interval 1	30 Sec	Hard	9 of 10
Rest Interval	90 sec	Easy	3 of 10
Interval 2	30 Sec	Hard	9 of 10
Rest Interval	90 Sec	Easy	3 of 10
Interval 3	30 Sec	Hard	9 of 10
Rest Interval	90 sec	Easy	3 of 10
Interval 4	30 Sec	Hard	9 of 10
Rest Interval	90 sec	Easy	3 of 10
Interval 5	30 Sec	Hard	9 of 10
Rest Interval	90 sec	Easy	3 of 10
Interval 6	30 Sec	Hard	9 of 10
Cool Down	5 Min	Cool	3 of 10

Day 2 - Stretch & Recovery Day

Equipment required: Bodyweight, Yoga Mat

GOLF Fitness:
Shed Pounds to **Shave Strokes**

	Stretch and Recovery
Mobility	Set 1
1) Three Plane Neck :30 seconds	
2) Shoulder Circles :30 seconds	
3) Fist Exercise :30 seconds	
4) Wrist Rotations :30 seconds	
5) Elbow Circles :30 seconds	
6) Egyptian :30 seconds	
7) Arm Circles :30 seconds	
8) Hula Hoop :30 seconds	
9) Ankle Circles :30 seconds	
10) Knee Circles :30 seconds	
Flexibility	Set 1
1) Toe Hang :30 seconds	
2) Cobra :30 seconds	
3) Spine Rotation w/ Club :30 seconds	
4) Head Turner :30 seconds (each side)	
5) Headache Buster :30 seconds (each side)	
6) Chest Stretch 1 :30 seconds (each side)	
7) Chest Stretch 2 :30 seconds (each side)	
8) Backswing Angel :30 seconds	
9) Wrist Flexion :30 seconds (each side)	
10) Shoulder Stretch :30 seconds (each side)	
11) Kneeling Hip Flexor :30 seconds (each side)	
12) Piriformis :30 seconds (each side)	
13) Seated Groin Stretch :30 seconds (each side)	
14) Calf Stretch :30 seconds (each side)	
Interval Program (Rest Day)	
Light activity (golf) or rest.	

Day 3 - Advanced Workout B

Equipment required: Dumbbells, Stability Ball, Bench, Medicine Ball

FOAM ROLLING (7-minutes)

While this is optional, it is highly recommended you foam roll. Foam rolling is like getting a massage. It relaxes and prepares your deep tissue and muscles for work. Below is the bare minimum amount of time I recommend. Preferably, I would like you to spend as long as possible foam rolling.

1A) Hamstrings :30 secs / side

1B) Calves :30 secs / side

1C) Quads :30 secs / side

1D) IT Band :30 secs / side

1E) Hip Flexors :30 secs / side

1F) Low Back :30 secs / side

1G) Upper Back / Traps :30 secs / side

Warm-Up (5-Minutes)

Go through the following with no rest between exercises. If you have a clock with a timer, you can use it to know when to switch to the next exercise.

2A) Torso Twists :60 seconds

2B) Side Bends :60 seconds

2C) Inchworms :60 seconds

2D) Superman Reaches :30 seconds

2E) Bodyweight Squats :60 seconds

2F) Straight Up Sit Up :30 seconds

Rest 1 minute and move on to the workout (3A).

Workout B (about 20-minutes)

Go through the following Superset with no rest between exercises.

3A) Reverse Lunge x 8 each leg

3B) Lateral Plank with Pushup x 20

Rest 1 minute & repeat 2 more times for a total of 3 supersets.

Go through the following Superset with no rest between exercises.

4A) DB Curl, Press on One Leg x 8

4B) Ball Superman x 10

Rest 1 minute & repeat 2 more times for a total of 3 supersets.

Go through the following Superset with no rest between exercises.

5A) Plank, feet on stability ball x 30 secs

5B) Medicine Ball Oblique Throw x 10

Rest 1 minute & repeat 2 more times for a total of 3 supersets.

Interval Workout B (about 20-minutes)
Perform the interval training directly after Workout A. This will ensure you get it done and can go about your regular activities without worrying about coming back to this.

- ✓ Choose from the following: Treadmill, Bicycle, Elliptical, Hills, Track, Stairs
- ✓ Warm-up for 4 minutes getting progressively more intense with time.
- ✓ Perform an interval by exercising for 30 seconds at a "harder than normal cardio" pace (at a 8/10 level of effort).
- ✓ Follow that with "active rest" for 90 seconds by exercising at a slow pace (at a subjective 3/10 level of effort).
- ✓ Repeat for a total of 6 intervals.
- ✓ Finish with 5 minutes of very low intensity (3/10) exercise for a cool-down.
- ✓ This workout takes approximately 20 minutes.

GOLF Fitness:
Shed Pounds to Shave Strokes

	Workout B / Advanced		
Foam Rolling (7-Minutes)	Side 1	Side 2	
1A) Hamstrings :30 secs / side			
1B) Calves :30 secs / side			
1C) Quads :30 secs / side			
1D) IT Band :30 secs / side			
1E) Hip Flexors :30 secs / side			
1F) Low Back :30 secs / side			
1G) Upper Back :30 secs / side			
Warm-Up (5-Minutes)	Set 1		
2A) Torso Twists :60 seconds			
2B) Side Bends :60 seconds			
2C) Inchworms :60 seconds			
2D) Superman Reaches :30 seconds			
2E) Bodyweight Squats :60 seconds			
2F) Straight Up Sit up :30 seconds			
Workout B (about 20-minutes)	Set 1	Set 2	Set 3
3A) Reverse Lunge x 8 each leg			
3B) Lateral Plank with Pushup x 20			
4A) DB Curl, Press on One Leg x 8			
4B) Ball Superman x 10 (hold 10 seconds each rep)			
5A) Plank, legs on stability ball x 30 secs			
5B) Medicine Ball Oblique Throw x 10			
Interval Program B (about 20-minutes)	Time	Type	Intensity
Warm Up	3 Min	Warm	3 of 10
Warm Up	1 Min	Warm	5 of 10
Interval 1	30 Sec	Hard	8 of 10
Rest Interval	90 sec	Easy	3 of 10
Interval 2	30 Sec	Hard	8 of 10
Rest Interval	90 Sec	Easy	3 of 10
Interval 3	30 Sec	Hard	8 of 10
Rest Interval	90 sec	Easy	3 of 10
Interval 4	30 Sec	Hard	8 of 10
Rest Interval	90 sec	Easy	3 of 10
Interval 5	30 Sec	Hard	8 of 10
Rest Interval	90 sec	Easy	3 of 10
Interval 6	30 Sec	Hard	8 of 10
Cool Down	5 Min	Cool	3 of 10

Day 4 - Stretch & Recovery Day

Equipment required: Bodyweight, Yoga Mat

GOLF Fitness:
Shed Pounds to **Shave Strokes**

	Stretch and Recovery
Mobility	Set 1
1) Three Plane Neck :30 seconds	
2) Shoulder Circles :30 seconds	
3) Fist Exercise :30 seconds	
4) Wrist Rotations :30 seconds	
5) Elbow Circles :30 seconds	
6) Egyptian :30 seconds	
7) Arm Circles :30 seconds	
8) Hula Hoop :30 seconds	
9) Ankle Circles :30 seconds	
10) Knee Circles :30 seconds	
Flexibility	Set 1
1) Toe Hang :30 seconds	
2) Cobra :30 seconds	
3) Spine Rotation w/ Club :30 seconds	
4) Head Turner :30 seconds (each side)	
5) Headache Buster :30 seconds (each side)	
6) Chest Stretch 1 :30 seconds (each side)	
7) Chest Stretch 2 :30 seconds (each side)	
8) Backswing Angel :30 seconds	
9) Wrist Flexion :30 seconds (each side)	
10) Shoulder Stretch :30 seconds (each side)	
11) Kneeling Hip Flexor :30 seconds (each side)	
12) Piriformis :30 seconds (each side)	
13) Seated Groin Stretch :30 seconds (each side)	
14) Calf Stretch :30 seconds (each side)	
Interval Program (Rest Day)	
Light activity (golf) or rest.	

Day 5 - Advanced Workout C

Equipment required: Stability Ball

FOAM ROLLING (7-minutes)

While this is optional, it is highly recommended you foam roll. Foam rolling is like getting a massage. It relaxes and prepares your deep tissue and muscles for work. Below is the bare minimum amount of time I recommend. Preferably, I would like you to spend as long as possible foam rolling.

1A) Hamstrings :30 secs / side

1B) Calves :30 secs / side

1C) Quads :30 secs / side

1D) IT Band :30 secs / side

1E) Hip Flexors :30 secs / side

1F) Low Back :30 secs / side

1G) Upper Back / Traps :30 secs / side

Warm-Up (5-Minutes)

Go through the following with no rest between exercises. If you have a clock with a timer, you can use it to know when to switch to the next exercise.

2A) Torso Twists :60 seconds

2B) Side Bends :60 seconds

2C) Inchworms :60 seconds

2D) Superman Reaches :30 seconds

2E) Bodyweight Squats :60 seconds

2F) Straight Up Sit Up :30 seconds

Rest 1 minute and move on to the workout (3A).

Workout C (about 16-minutes)

3A) Bodyweight Squat x 30

3B) Incline Pushup (hands on ball) x 20

3C) Plank x 60 second hold

3D) 1-Leg Hip Extension (foot on ball) x 8 each leg

3E) Ball Cobra (no weights) x 30 second hold

3F) Wall Squat Hold x 45 Second hold

3G) Ball Jack Knife x 15

3H) Squat Thrust w/Pushup x 8

Rest 1 minute & repeat 2 more times for a total of 3 supersets.

Foam Rolling (7-Minutes)	Workout C / Advanced		
	Side 1	Side 2	
1A) Hamstrings :30 secs / side			
1B) Calves :30 secs / side			
1C) Quads :30 secs / side			
1D) IT Band :30 secs / side			
1E) Hip Flexors :30 secs / side			
1F) Low Back :30 secs / side			
1G) Upper Back :30 secs / side			
Warm-Up (5-Minutes)	Set 1		
2A) Torso Twists :60 seconds			
2B) Side Bends :60 seconds			
2C) Inchworms :60 seconds			
2D) Superman Reaches :30 seconds			
2E) Bodyweight Squats :60 seconds			
2F) Straight Up Sit up :30 seconds			
Workout C (about 20-minutes)	Set 1	Set 2	Set 3
3A) Bodyweight Squat x 30			
3B) Incline Pushup (hands on ball) x 20			
3C) Plank x 60 second hold			
3D) 1-Leg Hip Extension (foot on ball) x 8 each leg			
3E) Ball Cobra (no weights) x 30 second hold			
3F) Wall Squat Hold x 45 Second hold			
3G) Ball Jack Knife x 15			
3H) Squat Thrust w/Pushup x 8			

Interval Program (Rest Day)

Play 9 Holes or Driving Range and Short Game practice.
Aim for two hours of practice or play.
If you play and are capable of walking the course, lighten your
bag so that you have the bare essentials.

If weather is not acceptable for golf, walking on a treadmill
will work fine.

Days 6 & 7 - Off Days

Equipment required: Golf Clubs, Treadmill, Bicycle, Mall

Most of us lead sedentary lifestyles. As golfers though, we have an off day activity we can plug in for at least 30 minutes of easy activity. Putting on the practice green, going to the driving range, walking nine holes all qualify as easy activity. Even riding in a cart and playing golf count as easy activity.

If you find you can't play golf due to cold weather or rain you may walk on a treadmill. Go to the mall and walk around. The key is getting off your butt and doing something. Stop watching the TV and move around.

Yoga and Pilates are good off day activities as well. Just don't overdo them, our workouts are going to be strenuous during the week.

The more overweight you are, the more you should focus on non-weight bearing activities. Swimming and bicycling are great activities.

Remember, it's an easy activity, it should NOT be intense.

Chapter Three: Is There Anything Else I Need To Know?

Last chapter we learned the techniques we will use to burn fat and perfect our new golf body. Think of these as the tools to sculpt your new golf body.

These tools may be different than what you are using now... and that's good a good thing. I've found that those who switch from long, slow, boring cardio to the new high intensity cardio and resistance training see big results, quickly. Simply, your body doesn't know what just happened and it must adapt.

A shock to the system.

Now that we know what works and why it works, we must apply this knowledge.

Getting started is pretty easy, and I have laid out a plan for you. In fact, if you are ready, skip to the Workouts Chapter and get started. However, some of you may have questions about the workouts and want a bit more understanding before you get started. Wrapping your head around a new workout plan is always a challenge. You want to understand all of the ins and outs of the program before starting.

I've found that most questions you may have right now have already been asked by my past clients.

When clients email in for help, I usually see the same questions over and over.

I've compiled the most frequent questions I receive and have placed them in the following four sections for your convenience:

Home Gym Primer
Resistance Training
Interval Training and Cardio
Range of Motion

And as always, if you have a question and need help, please contact me:
Ask a Question on Facebook @ facebook.com/getfitforgolf

Q: What do I need to start working out?

Answer:

The Shed Pounds to Shave Strokes program was designed to be done at home or the gym with a minimal amount of equipment. Preparing your home gym is affordable and easy. In fact, you can get by with the bare essentials if you are on a budget. Splurging just a bit can fit you nicely for any type of exercise needed. Below is a list of 7 pieces of must own equipment to get the most out of this golf fitness program. You may also workout in a gym, which will have most if not all of the equipment required.

1. Dumbbells - I prefer the hexagon ended dumbbells because they can be used for more complex movements in our advanced golfer workouts. A good range here is 10, 15, 20, 25 pounders for the Shed Pounds to Shave Strokes workouts. You most likely have some already. Another option are the Bowflex Selecttech dumbbells.

2. Swiss Ball – also called a stability ball. 65cm is a good size to get. This can be deflated and brought along with you on trips.

3. Yoga Mat – nothing fancy here and something not too thick. The thicker the mat, the harder it is to maintain balance. This is for stretching and exercises performed on the ground.

4. Exercise Bands – these may be purchased affordably from just about any athletic store. However, we highly recommend Bodylastics exercise bands, which come with a lifetime warranty and are highly portable for travel. These can be used instead of dumbbells for most exercises.

5. Foam Roller Kit. Any foam roller will do, but we found the Rumble Roller to work just fine for our needs.

OPTIONAL:

- • GymBoss Timer – Some exercises are timed and a good programmable timer is recommended. This is also available for iPhone, iPod and Android devices for cheap.

- • Medicine Balls – 5, 8, 10 pounds is good. Dumbbells can be substituted in lieu of medicine balls.

- • Adjustable Dumbbells such as those made by Bowflex. 5-55 lb range is perfect for this golf program. CAUTION: Bowflex Selecttech are GREAT as long as you don't get rough with them or do renegade rows. I've sent back so many handles I can't count. For affordability and durability I recommend the old iron dumbbells.

In addition to workout tools, you will need measurement tools. These will be used to assess your progress.

- • Buy a high quality digital or arm scale (like your doctor has). You can ignore ones that measure body fat, as these are not proven to be 100% accurate.
- • Buy a good set of calipers and tape measure. I recommend Slim Guide skinfold caliper and MyoTape. Both can be purchased affordably at Amazon.com.

As you can see, you can purchase all of the above items from the comfort of your own home and have them delivered quickly.

Q: What's the first thing I should do when starting Shed Pounds to Shave Strokes?

Answer:

Keep it simple and focus on three things only:

1. Recruit your friends, family, doctor. Join us @ facebook.com/getfitforgolf for added social support.

2. Focus on simple nutrition. Simple nutrition is eating natural, whole foods in place of processed foods. You can eat as much fruit and vegetables as you like. I've never know anyone to get fat on eating too many carrots. Vegetables such as broccoli, green beans, carrots, cucumbers. Fruit such as blueberries, apples, oranges. Lean proteins such as turkey, lean ground beef, and chicken. Fiber rich snacks such as almonds, and hummus (watch the pita chips and use carrots instead). Drink plenty of water, and you can even enjoy green tea and sugar free drinks.

3. Performing the exercises as prescribed. The program is designed to couple weight training and high intensity intervals to produce maximum results. One without the other makes for a very bland cocktail. You can't have a rum and coke without the rum (which reminds me, try to limit your alcohol intake during this program for max results).

Q: How much fat can I lose with Shed Pounds to Shave Strokes?

Answer:

Quite a bit. Most people on average lose 1 pound of body fat per week. Beginners who never exercise can lose up to 5 pounds a week. I like to see 1-3 pounds per week as a rule of thumb. The less fat you have, the more stubborn the fat will be to get off. If you are down to your last 10 pounds - really pay attention to your intensity levels. The high intensity cardio sessions are where we will burn this stubborn fat away.

Q: How fast can I lose fat with Shed Pounds to Shave Strokes?

Answer:

Health professionals and Doctors recommend losing fat at a rate of 1-2 pound per week. As mentioned above, beginners may be able to lose 5 pounds or more in a week. This isn't a realistic amount each week though. As you lose more fat, the less will come off and your numbers will slow down. However, by changing our workouts every 4 weeks, we will see progress.

You didn't put the weight on overnight, it will not come off overnight. Commit to the program and improve your nutrition. Creating long term habits will keep you lean well in to your golden years.

Q: Will Shed Pounds to Shave Strokes help me turn fat into muscle?
Answer:
No, this is a myth that is as old as Betty White. Shed Pounds to Shave Strokes will help you sculpt your body like an artist. The end result will be a lean athletic golf body. Not only will you feel and look better, you will play golf better.

Q: Why should I only use each workout level of Shed Pounds to Shave Strokes for 4 weeks?
Answer:
Re-read Chapter One for the specifics.

Only poor eating will halt your fat loss using our system. So if you aren't losing weight, check your nutrition carefully. Switching our workouts every four weeks will help you break through fat loss plateaus.

Q: When should I workout? Is it better to workout in the morning?

Answer:

It doesn't matter when you workout. It only matters that you workout.

Consistency is key to success with this program. So find a time when you can be alone and focus on your workouts. Eliminate all distractions.

Q: I work 45-65 hours per week and I have a young family. How do I fit exercise into my day?

Answer:

Get up early and before anyone else is up. Alternatively, do the workouts at night after the children are in bed.

It is important that you schedule your workouts as time for yourself. Pretend it's a very important appointment each day that can not be missed. After all, you are trying to lose weight to live longer in addition to improving your golf game right?

Q: Why should I do resistance training if I want to lose fat?

Answer:

Weight training will help you keep your muscle mass and even increase it during the Shed Pounds to Shave Strokes program. Without resistance the body may burn the muscles up for energy. Weight training puts a halt on this.

Finally, resistance training has been proven to improve the health of your cardiovascular system. Training with weights also increases your bone density.

Q: I was told that 15-20 repetitions would help me lose fat. Why does you have me using only 8 repetitions?
Answer:
The key difference here is intensity. Using a low weight and high reps does not force our body to adapt. We must challenge the muscles so they adapt, and as a result, contribute to fat loss. Light weights are not challenging and your body won't have to work hard or burn fat.

Q: I don't understand the format of the Shed Pounds to Shave Strokes workouts. Can you
explain what supersets are?
Answer:
Supersets are paired exercises done back to back. There is no rest when moving from exercise A to exercise B. However, we do rest after both exercise A and exercise B have been completed.

Here is an example superset taken from our Beginner Workout A:

Superset #1

1A) Pushup x 12
1B) Stick-up x 12

Rest 1 minute and repeat 2 more times.

The two exercises in this superset are Pushups and Stick-Ups. Perform 12 pushups then immediately do 12 stick-ups with no rest between. When you complete the Stick-Ups rest one minute, then perform this superset 2 more times starting with Pushups.

Q: For exercises where you do each side, if you list 8 repetitions, does that mean I do 8 reps on each side?
Answer:
Yes.

Q: What does tempo mean? What does the 2-0-1 mean?
Answer:
The numbers are seconds for each phase of a repetition.

2 - The first number means the lowering phase of the exercise. In this example, 2 seconds.

0 - This is the amount of time you would pause the weight in the lowest position. Such as a bench press when you lower the weight to your chest. 0 seconds would mean there is no pause.

1 - This is the lifting phase. Try to raise the weight back to the starting position in 1 second.

For example, in a pushup done with a 2-0-1 tempo, you would take 2 seconds to lower your body, 0 seconds to pause (no pause), and then one second to push yourself up.

Q: How much weight should I use?

Answer:

Pick a weight that allows you to get 1 more repetition than required. For example, if the workout asks for 8 repetitions - choose a weight that you can do 9 or 10 times. This would be a good weight for all 3 sets.

If you pick a weight you can only do 5 times, it's time to choose a lighter weight for your next set.

Alternatively, if you pick a weight you can do 12 or 15 times, you need to pick a heavier weight for your next set. Trial and error is the only way to find the proper weights to use.

Don't forget to write down the amount of weight you used for your exercises.

Q: Can I do my resistance training one day and interval training the next day?
Answer:
This if fine. I prefer to hammer them both out in the same workout so I can check that off my daily to do list though.

Again, if you have more time do both on the same day. If you are short on time, it is fine to break these apart.

Q: Can I lose fat from a specific area by doing certain exercises? What exercises will help me lose fat from my inner thighs and my love handles?
Answer:
No. Spot removal is a myth.

If I knew there was one secret for spot removal I would be rich... and I'm not.

The body is pre-set on where it stores fat and in what amounts. Conversely, bodybuilders frequently sculpt their muscles with specific body part workouts. Unfortunately fat doesn't work in this same manner. Muscles are controlled by voluntary movement and respond to stimuli. Fat just hangs around.

Doing one thousand crunches a day won't burn off your belly fat. In fact, you will just have bigger ab muscles under the fat making your belly stick out even more.

Here are 5 Fat Loss Tips from my good friend Craig Ballantyne:

1. Eat several small meals per day, rather than 2-3 large meals.
2. Monitor your food intake using fitday.com.
3. Determine how many calories you should eat per day to maintain your bodyweight.
4. If you want to lose fat, start by reducing your food intake by 200-300 calories per day below your maintenance level and add 3 workouts per week using the exercise techniques discussed below.
5. Stop eating processed foods and replace all sweetened beverages with water or Green Tea. This can quickly reduce your food intake by many, many calories.

Q: I see the Shed Pounds to Shave Strokes Workout schedule calls for 30 minutes of easy

activity on off days. What activities qualify for easy activities?

Answer:

Included in this program are Flexibility and Stretching routines to use on your off days. These will count as your easy activity. If you feel adventurous, you can use the stretching routines before before or first thing in the morning.

Most of us lead sedentary lifestyles. As golfers though, we have an off day activity we can plug in for this 30 minutes of easy activity. Putting on the practice green, going to the driving range, walking nine holes all qualify as easy activity. Even riding in a cart and playing golf count as easy activity.

If you find you can't play golf due to cold weather or rain you may walk on a treadmill. Go to the mall and walk around. The key is getting off your butt and doing something. Stop watching the TV and move around.

Yoga and Pilates are good off day activities as well. Just don't overdo them, our workouts are going to be strenuous.

The more overweight you are, the more you should focus on non-weight bearing activities. Swimming and bicycling are great activities.

Remember, it's an easy activity, it should NOT be intense.

Q: I do have two questions: First, you say don't go to failure on sets. Why? Second, for cardio (intervals), why the bike over running?
Answer:
Question 1: Safety first. You can hurt yourself lifting weights. Most don't have access to a spotter and going to failure is a recipe for disaster.

Another reason not to go to failure is that it's not going to help you much more than having 1 or 2 reps left in the tank. Stopping one rep short of failure will still give you the same benefits as going to failure, but without risking the chance of improper technique.

Question 2: Intervals on the bike are safer and more effective. You can't really fall off an exercise bike. I guess you can if you had too much to drink. But we won't be drinking and exercising at the same time.

Running outside you can step on a rock, step in a hole, or sprain a muscle if you don't take the time to properly warm up. Sprinting outside really does require an extensive warmup. If you are short on time, go with the bike.

Q: What is Interval Training?

Answer:

Short burst cardio workouts that burn more fat than long, slow, boring cardio routines. Interval training workouts begin with a warmup period, then move in to short bursts of activity, followed by a recovery period.

Best thing, these shorter workouts burn WAY more fat than traditional cardio. Even beginners can take to Interval Training immediately.

In each interval training workout, you'll be given an intensity level to reach. Here is a short guide to help you figure out the intensity levels I will prescribe on your interval workouts.

Level 1/10 – Standing still at rest

Level 3/10 – Recovery level – I.e. walking at a slow pace

Level 6/10 – Regular long, slow cardio pace

Level 7/10 – Beginner Interval Intensity

Level 8/10 – Intermediate Interval Intensity

Level 9/10 – Advanced Interval Intensity

Level 10/10 – Running for your life! (No need to do intervals at this pace, ever!)

NOTE: We do not use heart rate monitors for interval training. We work based on intensity as opposed to heart rate zones.

Interval Program 1 Example:
- ✓ Warm-up for 4 minutes getting progressively more intense with time.
- ✓ Perform an interval by exercising for 30 seconds at a "harder than normal cardio" pace (at a 7/10 level of effort).
- ✓ Follow that with "active rest" for 90 seconds by exercising at a slow pace (at a subjective 3/10 level of effort).
- ✓ Repeat for a total of 6 intervals.
- ✓ Finish with 5 minutes of very low intensity (3/10) exercise for a cool-down.
- ✓ This workout takes approximately 20 minutes.

Program 1 Interval Training (about 20-minutes)
Choose from the following: Treadmill, Bicycle, Elliptical, Hills, Track, Stairs
Level 3/10 Speed x 1-minute
Level 3/10 Speed x 1-minute
Level 3/10 Speed x 1-minute
Level 3/10 Speed x 1-minute
Level 7/10 x 30 Seconds

Level 3/10 x 1-minute 30 seconds

Level 7/10 x 30 Seconds

Level 3/10 x 1-minute 30 seconds

Level 7/10 x 30 Seconds

Level 3/10 x 1-minute 30 seconds

Level 7/10 x 30 Seconds

Level 3/10 x 1-minute 30 seconds

Level 7/10 x 30 Seconds

Level 3/10 x 1-minute 30 seconds

Level 7/10 x 30 Seconds

Level 3/10 Speed x 5-minutes

Let's say a beginner regularly walks at 3.5 mph on the treadmill for 20 minutes. That means they are exercising at a 6/10 level of intensity when they are walking at 3.5 mph. To take it up to level 7, simply increase the treadmill speed. our beginner would increase the treadmill speed to about 3.8 mph. Each interval only lasts 30 seconds. At the end of the 30 seconds they would drop it down to a level 3, which is walking at a slow pace.

You might need to go through a brief "trial and error" period in order to find the right intensity level for your interval training. However, always be CONSERVATIVE and do not exercise beyond your capacity. Train hard but SAFE.

Q: How is Interval Training different from cardio training?
Answer:
Interval training is a hybrid form of cardio training. It is very efficient and we use it primarily for fat loss in the Shed Pounds to Shave Strokes workouts.

Regular cardio training is generally performed at a slow and steady pace over a long period of time. Interval Training is simply short bursts of hard exercise followed by recovery periods. It is a good rule of thumb to rest 3 times the time exercised. For example, 30 seconds of hard work would be followed by 90 seconds of recovery at a level 3 on our intensity scale.

If you have ever done a spin class, you have done interval training. Instructors increase the cycling intensity for 30 seconds and then slow down for a minute or longer.

Q: Should I exercise in the fat burning zone to lose fat?
Answer:
The fat burning zone is another myth. There is no magical "fat burning zone".

Focus on intensity over time. You will get much better results in your fat loss.

Q: My friends said that it is best to do my cardio first thing in the morning and that will help me lose the most fat. Should I?

Answer:

Ignore the 'best time' to perform workouts for fat loss theory. The best workout is a workout you will actually do, at a time you are most likely to do it. Exercise when it fits your schedule and when you have the highest chance of completing a workout.

Q: How much cardio should I do each day?

Answer:

20-minutes of interval training should be more than adequate. Going beyond this is not really necessary for our purposes.

Beginners should use lower intensity and perform it in blocks of 5 minutes until they have built up to 20 to 30 minutes per day.

Q: If I have extra time is it O.K. to do 10 intervals instead of 6?

Answer:

No, 6 intervals are more than enough for our sessions. In fact, the more muscle you gain, the harder the intervals will become.

If you are exerting yourself as the interval workout charts recommend, you will be struggling to finish the 6th interval. If you are not having a hard time, you are not performing them with adequate intensity.

The more advanced your fitness, the more intense your workouts will be. If you are advanced, you will know that 6 high intensity intervals will be challenging.

Q: How many times a week can I do intervals?
Answer:
Let's set the maximum at 4 times per week. Again, if you are doing intervals at the end of each workout, that would be 3 interval sessions per week. If you want to improve your results, add a fourth day, but make sure you do no more than 4 interval sessions per week.

Make sure you have one full day off per week from all intense exercise.

Q: What is the best equipment to use for interval training?
Answer:

1.   Stationary cycle or spin bike
2.   Treadmill

Treadmill sprinting will yield the best results. However, treadmills have dangers that are not worth risking. In fact, I've been running on treadmills when the belt slips or the power completely goes off.

If you have knee or shin splint issues, avoid a treadmill.

Therefore, stick with a stationary cycle if you have access to one. Adjusting the intensity level is easy. Just turn up the resistance and pedal harder. Aim for 80-100 RPM to be achieved during the work interval. Choosing the stationary bike is the safe choice. If you find the results are lacking, switch your method over to the treadmill.

Q: How does interval training work? Is it based on heart rate zones?
Answer:
No. Interval training does not bring heart rate zones in to play. Interval training is based on intensity. How hard can you work for 30 seconds? Trust me on this, by the 6th interval, your heart rate will be racing.

Further, no research has proven that maintaining a certain heart rate aid in fat loss.

Remember that your intervals will be performed at an intensity that you couldn't maintain for long periods of time.

Q: I've decided to use a stationary bike for my intervals. Do I keep the resistance the same and go faster or just increase the resistance and pedal the same?
Answer:
You would increase the resistance until you reach your intensity goal. Most stationary bikes have knobs or settings you can use to adjust the resistance. This may require you to pedal harder to achieve your interval level.

You can get a great interval workout with any machine as long as you follow the interval intensity targets and time intervals.

Q: What about using the jump rope for intervals?
Answer:
This is great. Just make sure you adjust your intensity per the interval workout charts. I love doing the jump rope and then walking around a basketball court for my rest interval.

Q: What is Range of Motion?

Answer:

Range of motion is simply the range your joints, muscles, and connective tissues allow you to move. If your muscles are tight, you have reduced range of motion. The same goes for your connective tissues such as ligaments and tendons. Your joints can also be stiff from lack of use. By applying a specific stretching and range of motion workout we have restore the proper movement to your body. However, this can take time and patience.

Q: What is Joint Mobility?

Answer:

Joint Mobility is the first building block to a successful workout program. The goal of Joint Mobility is to pump fresh synovial fluid into the joint and reduce resistance. Basically, a joint mobility program greases the wheels of motion. If you've been static and not moved much, your joints might feel old and stiff. You can get rid of this by doing a daily Joint Mobility routine. A good program starts at your neck and moves all the way down the body hitting all the major joints.

Q: How Many Reps Should I Do for Joint Mobility?

Answer:

Good question and I generally recommend reps based on your age. If you are 30, do 30 reps of each Joint Mobility exercise. You can also just do what feels good to you. If 10 feels good and the joint is nice and smooth stop there.

Q: So what is Foam Rolling?

Answer:

SMR is performed with a foam roller to break up adhesions formed by your muscles. Adhesions can form from overuse, improper use, or injury that reduce your range of motions. The adhesions actually form to prevent further injury. The adhesions form across the muscle and restrict the muscle from working properly. A foam roller allows you to massage adhesions and break them down so the muscle is nice and straight. When the muscle is nice and connected again without adhesions your range of motion is restored.

Your own bodyweight is used against the firmness of the foam roller to massage knotted muscles back to normal. Essentially, you are trying to break down the adhesion to restore normal musculature.

Q: How do I foam roll?

Answer:

SMR could not be simpler. Basically you use gravity and your own bodyweight to apply pressure to knots in your muscles. You roll out until you feel discomfort in your muscle.

Once you have reached a pain point, you hold yourself in position and let gravity do its work. The muscle will eventually relax and release and you will feel a reduction in pain. A good rule of thumb is to allow at least 30 seconds on the spot or until you feel the muscle actually relax.

Q: How long should I hold a stretch?

Answer:

Aim for at least 20 seconds up to 60 seconds. You want to make sure you stretch a little bit further than the day before. Stop if you feel a sharp pain, that is too much of a stretch and you could injure yourself.

Chapter Four: How Do I Perform the Exercises?

Foam Rolling / Trigger Point

Foam Rolling is used as a self-massage method to help break up scar tissue that is built up over time while training. To help break up the scar tissue so blood can freely flow better to your muscles and help transport out toxins and acid build up, we roll over our muscle using a foam roller.

This will help improve mobility and recovery a ton!

This may be painful at the start but it is ESSENTIAL for improved performance and results!

Focus on rolling over the most tender areas on your body. A good rule of thumb is to do at least 10 passes over each of the areas described and pictured below.

Hamstrings

1. Start right under your glute and continue to roll all the way down to just above the back of your knee.
2. Rotate your leg side to side to expose more tender areas.

Calves

1. Start under your knee and continue to roll all the way down to your Achilles tendon.

2. Cross one leg over the top of the other to increase amount of pressure.

3. Rotate legs side to side to expose more tender areas.

Quads

1. Lay off to the side of the roller and start right at your hip flexor and roll all the way down to the top of your knee.

2. Rotate side to side to expose more tender areas.

IT Band

1. This is one of the biggest problem areas for most people – It will be painful! Pay extra attention to this area.

2. Roll on your side starting just above your knee and roll all the way up to your hip.

3. Roll side to side to expose more tender areas.

Hip Flexors

1. Start off to the side of the roller at an angle.

2. Roll over your hip flexors.

3. Rotate side to side to expose more tender areas.

Low Back

1. Start by sitting on your butt then roll back onto the roller either rolled over to the left or right side.

2. DO NOT roll directly over your spine.

3. Roll over your low back from the top of your glute up to your lats.

Upper Back / Traps

1. Starting on your upper back, raise your arms and point them to the ceiling to spread out your scapula to expose tender spots.

2. Roll side to side to hit other areas.

3. Roll up to your traps down to the bottom of your lats. You can also cross one arm over your chest to expose even more tender spots.

Warm Up

Perform this warmup before your workout. Properly warming up will allow your body to loosen up and reduce injury while improving performance.

Torso Twists

1. Stand with feet shoulder width apart.

2. Place a golf club on shoulders behind your neck and hang on to club with hands.

3. Rotate to the left and right, allowing your heel to come off ground.

4. Rotate left at a 90 degree angle and then back to the right.

Side Bends

1.   Stand with feet shoulder width apart.

2.   Extend arms directly above head and tilt to the right, and then to your left.

3.   It is important to stay 'stacked' and not let your body tilt forward or backwards.

Inchworms

1. Stand with feet together.

2. From a standing position with your feet together or slightly apart, engage ("brace") your abdominal muscles to stabilize your spine.

3. Gently exhale and bend forward from your hips ("hip hinging"). Try to keep your knees straight (but not locked). Slowly lower your torso towards the floor until you can place your fingers or palms of your hands on the floor in front of your body. If your hamstrings are tight, you may need to bend your knees slightly. Try to keep the spine flat.

4. Slowly begin to walk your hands forward, away from your feet. Your heels will begin to rise off the floor. Continue walking your hands forward until you reach a full-push-up position where your spine,

hips and head are level with the floor (plank position)

5. Slowly begin walking your feet forward towards your hands, taking steps without moving your hands. Maintain a flat spine throughout and continue walking until your feet are close to your hands.

Superman Reaches

1. Starting Position: Lie on your stomach on a mat or the floor with your legs outstretched behind you. Your toes are pointing toward the wall behind you. Reach your arms out overhead with your palms facing each other. Relax your neck and align your head with your spine.

2.   Upward Phase: Exhale. Deepen your abdominal and core muscles to stabilize your spine and slowly and strongly reach both legs away from your torso until they lift a few inches off the floor. At the same time float both arms a few inches off the floor. Keep both legs and arms straight and allow any rotation in the arms, legs, shoulders or pelvis. Your head is aligned with your spine. Do not allow your head to lift up or to droop toward the floor. Do not allow the back to arch. Hold this position briefly.

3.   Downward Phase: Gently inhale and lower your legs and arms back to your starting position without any movement in your low back or hips.

Bodyweight Squats

1. Stand with your feet just greater than shoulder-width apart.

2. Start the movement at the hip joint. Push your hips backward and "sit back into a chair". Make your hips go back as far as possible.

3. Squat as deep as possible, but keep your low back tensed in a neutral position.

4. Don't let your lower back become rounded.

5. Push with your glutes, hamstrings, and quadriceps to return to the start position.

Straight Up Sit up

1. Lay flat on back, arms extended behind head and on floor.

2. Legs remain flat.

3. Reach up and try to touch the ceiling while contracting your abs.

4. Lower back down and lower arms back to ground.

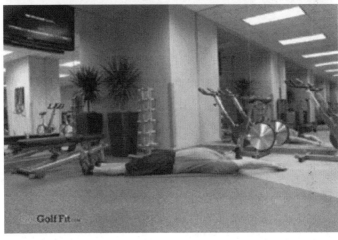

Beginner Workout Exercises

Exercises are listed in the order you perform them during the workout for your ease of use.

Workout A

Beginner Workout A

T-Squat

1.   Muscles: Rhomboids (upper back), quadriceps (front of thighs), hamstrings, butt.
2.   Hold your hands straight out to your sides in a "T" formation at all times.
3.   Keep your upper back and shoulders tensed throughout the exercise.
4.   Stand with your feet just greater than shoulder-width apart.
5.   Start the movement at the hip joint. Push your hips backward and "sit back into a chair". Make your hips go back as far as possible.
6.   Squat as deep as possible, but keep your low back tensed in a neutral position.
7.   Push with your glutes, hamstrings, and quadriceps to return to the start position.

121

Stick-up

1. Muscles: Rhomboids (upper back), posterior deltoids (shoulders)

2. Stand with your back against a wall. Your feet should be 6 inches away from the wall and your butt, upper back, and head should all be in contact with the wall at all times in the exercise.

3. Stick your hands up overhead. Try to keep your shoulders, elbows, and wrists in contact with the wall at all times.

4. Slide your arms down the wall and tuck your elbows into your sides. This should bring your shoulder blades down and together. You should feel a strong contraction in the muscles between your shoulder blades as well as the shoulder muscles.

5. Again, try to keep everything in contact with the wall.

6. From the bottom position, try to slowly slide your arms up until they are straight and in a "stick-em up" position. Again, try to keep everything in contact with the wall.

7. Try to improve your range of motion in this exercise each week.

8. The goal is to improve shoulder mobility and postural control.

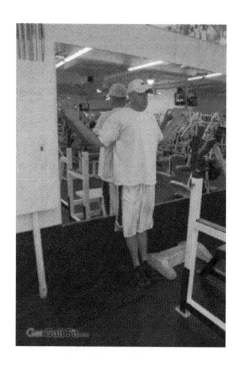

Single Leg Golf Posture Rotations

1. Stand upright and place your body in a proper address position, knees slightly bent, fixed spine angle, and arms crossed over your chest.

2. Raise the right foot slightly off the floor while maintaining your address position and fixed spine angle.

3. Begin to slowly rotate your shoulders to the right to the point of a complete shoulder turn.

4. Return to the starting position of the exercise and repeat.

5. Repeat the exercise balancing on the left foot.

Pushup

1. Keep the abs braced and body in a straight line from toes/knees to shoulders.

2. Place the hands on the floor slightly wider than shoulder-width apart.

3. Slowly lower yourself down until you are an inch off the ground.

4. Push through your chest, shoulders and triceps to return to the start position.

5. Keep your body in a straight line at all times.

6. If you have difficulty, try this from your knees.

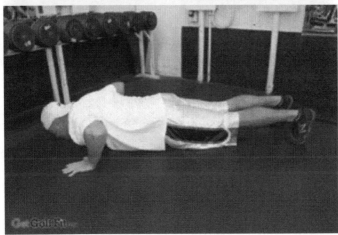

Lying Hip Extension

1. Muscles: Butt, hamstrings (back of thighs)

2. Lie on your back with your knees bent and feet flat on the floor.

3. Brace your abs, and contract your glutes (butt muscles) as if you were squeezing something between your cheeks.

4. Bridge your hips up by contracting your glutes. Don't use your lower back.

5. Hold your hips elevated for a 1-count. Keep your abs braced and squeeze the glutes.

6. Slowly lower your hips down until they are an inch above the ground. Then repeat.

Plank

1. Lie on your stomach on a mat.

2. Raise your body in a straight line and rest your bodyweight on your elbows and toes so that your body hovers over the mat.

3. Keep your back straight and your hips up. Hold (brace) your abs tight. Contract them as if someone was about to punch you in the stomach, but breath normally.

4. Hold this position for the recommended amount of time.

Workout B

Beginner Workout B Exercise Library

Exercises are listed below in the order you perform them during the workout.

Y-Squat

1. Muscles: Rhomboids (upper back), quadriceps (front of thighs), hamstrings, butt.
2. Hold your hands over your head in a "Y" formation at all times.
3. Keep your upper back and shoulders tensed throughout the exercise.
4. Stand with your feet just greater than shoulder-width apart.
5. Start the movement at the hip joint. Push your hips backward and "sit back into a chair". Make your hips go back as far as possible.
6. Squat as deep as possible, but keep your low back tensed in a neutral position.
7. Push with your glutes, hamstrings, and quadriceps to return to the start position.

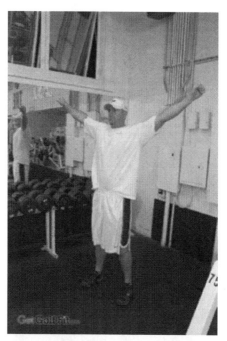

Cross Crawl

1. This is a combination warm-up and ab exercise.

2. Stand with your feet shoulder width-apart and hands straight overhead.

3. Slowly bring your opposite knee and elbow together in front of you.

4. Alternate sides.

Single Leg Reaching Lunge

1. Stand with your feet shoulder-width apart in front of a small object that you have placed 3 feet in front of you.

2. Now stand on your right leg, balance yourself, and then bend your knee and reach forward to touch the object with your right hand.

3. Touch the object and return to the starting position without losing your balance.

4. Without switching legs, perform the same exercise but use your left hand to reach forward and touch the cone.

5. Perform all repetitions on the right leg and then switch.

6. As you get better, you can place 3 cones in a line (one to the left, one in the center, and one to the right). This will require greater balance.

Incline Pushup

1. Keep the abs braced and body in a straight line from toes/knees to shoulders.

2. Place the hands on a bench or chair slightly wider than shoulder-width apart. Feet remain on ground.

3. Slowly lower yourself down until you are an inch off the ground.

4. Push through your chest, shoulders and triceps to return to the start position.

5. Keep your body in a straight line at all times.

6. If you have difficulty, try this from your knees.

Floor Cobra

1.   Lie prone on the floor. Stretch your legs back, tops of the feet on the floor. Spread your hands on the floor under your shoulders. Hug the elbows back into your body.

2.   Press the tops of the feet and thighs and the pubis firmly into the floor.

3.   On an inhalation, begin to straighten the arms to lift the chest off the floor, going only to the height at which you can maintain a connection through your pubis to your legs. Press the tailbone toward the pubis and lift the pubis toward the navel. Narrow the hip points. Firm but don't harden the buttocks.

4.   Firm the shoulder blades against the back, puffing the side ribs forward. Lift through the top of the

sternum but avoid pushing the front ribs forward, which only hardens the lower back. Distribute the backbend evenly throughout the entire spine.

Side Plank

1. Muscles: Abs, obliques, low back, shoulder

2. Lie on a mat on your side.

3. Support your bodyweight with your knees and on your right elbow.

4. Raise your body in a straight line so that your body hovers over the mat.

5. Keep your back straight and your hips up. Hold your abs tight. Contract them as if someone was about to punch you in the stomach, but breath normally.

Workout C

Beginner Workout C Exercise Library

Exercises are listed below in the order you perform them during the workout.

Prisoner Squat

1. Stand with your feet just greater than shoulder-width apart.

2. Clasp your hands behind your head. Keep your elbows back and shoulder blades pulled together to work the upper back.

3. Start the movement at the hip joint. Push your hips backward and "sit back into a chair." Make your hips go back as far as possible.

4. Squat as deep as possible, but keep your low back tensed in a neutral position.

5. Do not round your lower back.

6. Push with your glutes, hamstrings, and quadriceps to return to the start position.

Pushup

1. Keep the abs braced and body in a straight line from toes/knees to shoulders.

2. Place the hands on the floor slightly wider than shoulder-width apart.

3. Slowly lower yourself down until you are an inch off the ground.

4. Push through your chest, shoulders and triceps to return to the start position.

5. Keep your body in a straight line at all times.

6. If you have difficulty, try this from your knees.

Plank

1.   Lie on your stomach on a mat.

2.   Raise your body in a straight line and rest your bodyweight on your elbows and toes so that your body hovers over the mat.

3.   Keep your back straight and your hips up. Hold (brace) your abs tight. Contract them as if someone was about to punch you in the stomach, but breath normally.

4.   Hold this position for the recommended amount of time.

Lying 1-Leg Hip Extension

1. Muscles: Butt, hamstrings (back of thighs)
2. Lie on your back with your knees bent and feet flat on the floor.
3. Brace your abs, and contract your right glute (butt muscle) while you take your left leg, lift it off the floor and hold it in the position shown.
4. Using the right glute, bridge your hips up.
5. Keep your abs braced. Do not use your low back to do this exercise.
6. Slowly lower your hips down until they are an inch above the ground.
7. Perform all reps for one leg and then switch sides

Side Plank

1.   Muscles: Abs, obliques, low back, shoulder

2.   Lie on a mat on your side.

3.   Support your bodyweight with your knees and on your right elbow.

4.   Raise your body in a straight line so that your body hovers over the mat.

5.   Keep your back straight and your hips up. Hold your abs tight. Contract them as if someone was about to punch you in the stomach, but breath normally.

Wall Squat

1. Stand against a wall with your feet just greater than shoulder-width apart.

2. Place your feet 12-18 inches in front of the wall.

3. Start the movement at the hip joint. Lower your hips down until your thighs are parallel to the floor.

4. Push with your glutes, hamstrings, and quadriceps to return to the start position.

Horse Reach

1. Begin this exercise by placing your hands and knees on the floor.

2. Place your hands directly under your shoulders with your knees directly under your hips (as in the photo on Page 1).

3. Your back remains flat with eyes focused on the floor. Visualize balancing a glass of water in the middle of your lower back. No spilling!

4. From this position, simultaneously extend your left arm and right leg to positions that are directly out in front and behind the torso, respectively.

5. Throughout the extension of your arm and leg, maintain a flat back position. Keep balancing that glass of water on your lower back.

6. Once both the arm and leg are extended, hold the position for two seconds and then return to the starting position.

7. Repeat this sequence with the opposite arm and leg.

Stick-up

1. Muscles: Rhomboids (upper back), posterior deltoids (shoulders)

2. Stand with your back against a wall. Your feet should be 6 inches away from the wall and your butt, upper back, and head should all be in contact with the wall at all times in the exercise.

3. Stick your hands up overhead. Try to keep your shoulders, elbows, and wrists in contact with the wall at all times.

4. Slide your arms down the wall and tuck your elbows into your sides. This should bring your shoulder blades down and together. You should feel a strong contraction in the muscles between your shoulder blades as well as the shoulder muscles.

5. Again, try to keep everything in contact with the wall.

6. From the bottom position, try to slowly slide your arms up until they are straight and in a "stick-em up" position. Again, try to keep everything in contact with the wall.

7. Try to improve your range of motion in this exercise each week.

8. The goal is to improve shoulder mobility and postural control.

Intermediate Workout Exercises

Exercises are listed in the order you perform them during the workout for your ease of use.

Workout A

Intermediate Workout A

Exercises are listed below in the order you perform them during the workout.

DB Chest Press

1. Muscles: Chest, triceps, shoulders
2. Lie on a flat bench.
3. Hold the dumbbells above your chest with your palms turned toward your feet.
4. Lower the dumbbells out and down to chest level.
5. Press the dumbbells up and in above the chest.

DB Row

1. Muscles: Lats, rhomboids (upper back), biceps, forearms, abs

2. Rest the left hand and left knee on a flat bench, lean over and keep the back flat.

3. Hold the dumbbell in the right hand in full extension.

4. Slowly row the dumbbell up to your lower abdomen.

5. Keep the low back tensed in a neutral position and the elbow tight to the side.

DB (Dumbbell) Squat

Muscles: Quadriceps (front of thighs), hamstrings (back of thighs), butt, forearms

1. Stand with your feet just greater than shoulder-width apart.

2. Start the movement at the hip joint. Push your hips backward and "sit back".

3. Squat as deep as possible, but keep your low back tensed in a neutral position.

4. Push with your glutes, hamstrings, and quadriceps to return to the start position.

5. For the dumbbell squat, hold a dumbbell in each hand on the outside of your legs.

6. Keep your low back arched. Do NOT round your low back.

159

Single-Leg Dumbbell Curl

1.   Grab one dumbbell for each hand and stand at attention.

2.   Slowly lift one of your legs off of the ground. You don't have to lift the leg very high, just enough so that if you lose your balance you can easily put it down to stop yourself from falling over.

3.   Alternate curls between arms.

4.   Halfway through your set, pause your curls and balance on your other leg.

5.   Complete the total number of repetitions.

Stability Ball Leg Curl

Muscles: Hamstrings, butt, calves (back of legs)

1. Lie on your back with the soles of your feet on a medium-sized Stability Ball.

2. Brace your abs, and contract your glutes (butt muscles) as if you were squeezing something between your cheeks. Bridge your hips up by contracting your glutes.

3. Keep your abs braced and contract your hamstrings and slowly curl the ball back towards your hips while keeping your hips bridged.

4. Pause and slowly return the ball to the start position while keeping the hips bridged.

Plank

1. Lie on your stomach on a mat.

2. Raise your body in a straight line and rest your bodyweight on your elbows and toes so that your body hovers over the mat.

3. Keep your back straight and your hips up. Hold (brace) your abs tight. Contract them as if someone was about to punch you in the stomach, but breath normally.

4. Hold this position for the recommended amount of time.

Workout B

Intermediate Workout B

Exercises are listed below in the order you perform them during the workout.

DB Step-Up to Balance

1. Muscles: Quadriceps (front of thighs), hamstrings (back of thighs), butt
2. Stand facing a bench. Place one foot on the bench and the other on the floor.
3. Hold dumbbells in hands at sides.
4. With your abs braced and glutes squeezed, start the movement by pushing through the bench foot to lift the body up to the standing position.
5. Lower your body under control. Pause briefly at the bottom and repeat.
6. Complete all reps for one side.

Dumbbell Woodchop

1. Stand with feet shoulder-width apart, holding a 5-pound dumbbell in front of your torso with both hands.

2. Engage your abs, keep shoulders down, and squat, bringing dumbbell toward right foot.

3. Stand up, using your abs and glutes, while lifting dumbbell diagonally across your body to left shoulder.

4. Switch sides (starting to left) and repeat.

Walkout Pushup

1. Stand with feet together.

2. From a standing position with your feet together or slightly apart, engage ("brace") your abdominal muscles to stabilize your spine.

3. Gently exhale and bend forward from your hips ("hip hinging"). Try to keep your knees straight (but not locked). Slowly lower your torso towards the floor until you can place your fingers or palms of your hands on the floor in front of your body. If your hamstrings are tight, you may need to bend your knees slightly. Try to keep the spine flat.

4. Slowly begin to walk your hands forward, away from your feet. Your heels will begin to rise off the floor. Continue walking your hands forward until you reach a full-push-up position where your spine, hips and head are level with the floor (plank position)

Cross Crawl

1. This is a combination warm-up and ab exercise.
2. Stand with your feet shoulder width-apart and hands straight overhead.
3. Slowly bring your opposite knee and elbow together in front of you.
4. Alternate sides.

Floor Cobra

1. Lie prone on the floor. Stretch your legs back, tops of the feet on the floor. Spread your hands on the floor under your shoulders. Hug the elbows back into your body.

2. Press the tops of the feet and thighs and the pubis firmly into the floor.

3. On an inhalation, begin to straighten the arms to lift the chest off the floor, going only to the height at which you can maintain a connection through your pubis to your legs. Press the tailbone toward the

175

pubis and lift the pubis toward the navel. Narrow the hip points. Firm but don't harden the buttocks.

4. Firm the shoulder blades against the back, puffing the side ribs forward. Lift through the top of the sternum but avoid pushing the front ribs forward, which only hardens the lower back. Distribute the backbend evenly throughout the entire spine.

Side Plank

1. Muscles: Abs, obliques, low back, shoulder

2. Lie on a mat on your side.

3. Support your bodyweight with your knees and on your right elbow.

4. Raise your body in a straight line so that your body hovers over the mat.

5. Keep your back straight and your hips up. Hold your abs tight. Contract them as if someone was about to punch you in the stomach, but breath normally.

Workout C

Intermediate Workout C

Exercises are listed below in the order you perform them during the workout.

Prisoner Squat

1. Stand with your feet just greater than shoulder-width apart.

2. Clasp your hands behind your head. Keep your elbows back and shoulder blades pulled together to work the upper back.

3. Start the movement at the hip joint. Push your hips backward and "sit back into a chair." Make your hips go back as far as possible.

4. Squat as deep as possible, but keep your low back tensed in a neutral position.

5. Do not round your lower back.

6. Push with your glutes, hamstrings, and quadriceps to return to the start position.

Decline Pushup

1. Keep the abs braced and body in a straight line from toes (knees) to shoulders.

2. Place the hands on the floor slightly wider than shoulder-width apart.

3. Elevate your feet onto a chair.

4. Take 5 seconds to lower yourself down until you are 2 inches off the ground.

5. Push through your chest, shoulders and triceps to return to the start position.

6. Keep your body in a straight line at all times.

Side Plank

1. Muscles: Abs, obliques, low back, shoulder
2. Lie on a mat on your side.
3. Support your bodyweight with your knees and on your right elbow.
4. Raise your body in a straight line so that your body hovers over the mat.
5. Keep your back straight and your hips up. Hold your abs tight. Contract them as if someone was about to punch you in the stomach, but breath normally.

Stability Ball Hip Extension

Muscles: Hamstrings, butt, calves (back of legs)

1. Lie on your back with the soles of your feet on a medium-sized Stability Ball.

2. Brace your abs, and contract your glutes (butt muscles) as if you were squeezing something between your cheeks. Bridge your hips up by contracting your glutes.

3. Slowly lower your hips down until they are an inch above the ground.

Ball Cobra

1. Lie with ball under mid-section; feet pointed toward floor and legs straight.

2. Extend arms in front of ball.

3. Draw-in belly button and squeeze butt muscles.

4. Pinch shoulder blades back and down to bring arms around to side of body.

5. Return arms to front of body.

Wall Squat

1. Stand against a wall with your feet just greater than shoulder-width apart.

2. Place your feet 12-18 inches in front of the wall.

3. Start the movement at the hip joint. Lower your hips down until your thighs are parallel to the floor.

4. Push with your glutes, hamstrings, and quadriceps to return to the start position.

Horse Reach

1. Begin this exercise by placing your hands and knees on the floor.

2. Place your hands directly under your shoulders with your knees directly under your hips (as in the photo on Page 1).

3. Your back remains flat with eyes focused on the floor. Visualize balancing a glass of water in the middle of your lower back. No spilling!

4. From this position, simultaneously extend your left arm and right leg to positions that are directly out in front and behind the torso, respectively.

5. Throughout the extension of your arm and leg, maintain a flat back position. Keep balancing that glass of water on your lower back.

6. Once both the arm and leg are extended, hold the position for two seconds and then return to the starting position.

7. Repeat this sequence with the opposite arm and leg.

Squat Thrusts NO Pushup

1. Start in the top of the pushup position with your abs braced.

2. Thrust your knees in towards your chest and then back out quickly.

3. Repeat.

189

Advanced Workout Exercises

Exercises are listed in the order you perform them during the workout for your ease of use.

Workout A

Advanced Workout A

Exercises are listed below in the order you perform them during the workout.

Single Leg Dumbbell Squat

1. Standing up, holding dumbbells at your side.
2. Lift your left leg slightly off the ground and balance on your right leg.
3. Squat down on your right leg and maintain control.
4. Keep your right knee behind your toes.
5. Do not allow your right thigh to go beyond parallel. Maintain left foot off the ground.
6. Perform all reps on right side before performing on the left side.

DB Warrior Row

1.   1.   With knees bent and back arched, hold two dumbbells at your side.

2.   2.   Pull both straight up to the sides.

3.   3.   Keep your elbows out to the sides and exhale on the way up.

4.   4.   Return slowly to the floor.

5.   5. "Pull" the weight with the latissimus dorsi muscles (the "wings")

Mistakes
- ¥   Cocking the head up
- ¥   Shrugging the shoulders as you pull the dumbbells
- ¥   Bending the wrists as you pull the dumbbells

DB Stability Ball Press

1. To perform the exercise, begin with the dumbbells in your hands and maneuver into a "bridge" position on the stability ball. Your head, neck and upper back should be balanced on top of the ball. Keep your feet firmly on the ground and your hips up straight.

2. Start with the dumbbells up, arms straight. Slowly lower the dumbbells to the sides of your chest, bending at the elbows and then return them to the top.

3. To get the most from the exercise, be sure not to drop the hips or twist the torso while performing the movement. Always perform a good warm-up before doing any exercise or stretch.

Dumbbell Squat, Curl, Press

1. Stand with your feet just greater than shoulder-width apart.

2. Hold two dumbbells at your sides.

3. Start the movement at the hip joint. Push your hips backward and "sit back into a chair". Make your hips go back as far as possible.

4. Squat as deep as possible, but keep your low back tensed in a neutral position.

5. Don't let your lower back become rounded.

6. Push with your glutes, hamstrings, and quadriceps to return to the start position.

7. After reaching the start position for your squat, curl both dumbbells.

8. Your palms should be facing toward your shoulders when you reach the top position for your curl.

9. When the dumbbells have reached your shoulders, press both overhead at the same time.

10. Your palms will naturally want to rotate forward. This is fine and what we want.

11. Lower weights back down to shoulders and reverse the curl.

12. Repeat.

199

Prone Twister with Stability Ball

1. Start in a full push-up position with palms on floor aligned under shoulders, feet on a stability ball.

2. Lower feet until they're grasping the sides of the ball.

3. Keeping upper body stationary, rotate your legs and hips to the left in 2 counts; return to center and rotate to the right in 2 counts.

4. To modify, place your knees on either side of the ball.

Medicine Ball Slam

1. To complete this forceful throw, begin standing with feet shoulder-width apart with a medicine ball held over your head with both hands.

2. Bring your arms down the front of your body towards your hips.

3. Release the ball once your arms are almost completely lowered, throwing it down onto the floor directly between your feet.

4. Catch the ball as it bounces up towards you.

Picture pending.

Workout B

Advanced Workout B

Exercises are listed below in the order you perform them during the workout.

Reverse Lunge

Muscles: Hamstrings (back of thighs), butt, quadriceps (front of thighs),

1. Stand with your feet shoulder-width apart. Hold DB's in each hand.
2. Brace your abs, and contract your glutes (butt muscles) as if you were squeezing something between your cheeks.
3. Step backward with left leg, resting the toe on the ground.
4. Squat straight down with the right leg supporting the body weight. Lower yourself until your right thigh is parallel to the floor.
5. Return to the start position by pushing with the muscles of the right leg. Focus on pushing with glutes and hamstrings. Do all reps on one side then switch.

Lateral Plank with Pushup

1. Keep your abs braced and body in a straight line from toes to shoulders.

2. Place the hands on the floor slightly wider than shoulder-width apart, BUT place one hand in front of shoulder level and the other hand behind shoulder level.

3. Slowly lower yourself down until you are 1 inch off the ground.

4. Push through your chest, shoulders and triceps to return to the start position.

5. Keep your body in a straight line at all times.

6. Alternate sides.

Single-Leg Dumbbell Curl to Press

1. Grab one dumbbell for each hand and stand at attention.

2. Slowly lift one of your legs off of the ground. You don't have to lift the leg very high. Lift just enough so that if you lose your balance you can easily put it down to stop yourself from falling over.

3. Curl the dumbbell up and then press straight over head. Perform this under control and maintain your balance.

4. Alternate curl to press between arms.

5. Halfway through your set, pause your curl to press and balance on your other leg.

6. Complete the total number of repetitions.

208

Ball Superman

1. Lie with ball under mid-section; feet pointed toward floor and legs straight.

2. Extend arms in front of ball.

3. Draw-in belly button and squeeze butt muscles.

4. Pinch shoulder blades back and down to bring arms around to side of body.

5. Move arms to front of body like you are flying.

6. Return arms to starting position and repeat.

Plank, Feet on Stability Ball

1.   Lie on your stomach on a mat.

2.   Raise your body in a straight line and rest your bodyweight on your hands. Place the tips of your toes on top of a stability ball.

3.   Keep your back straight and your hips up. Hold (brace) your abs tight. Contract them as if someone was about to punch you in the stomach, but breath normally.

4.   Hold this position for the recommended amount of time.

Medicine Ball Oblique Throw

1. Start in a wide athletic stance with a good bend in your knees. Hold the medicine ball in both hands in front of you.

2. Throw the medicine ball against the wall at about chest height.

3. Catch the ball off of the wall rotate to the opposite hip and throw then throw the ball back.

Workout C

Advanced Workout C

Exercises are listed below in the order you perform them during the workout.

Bodyweight Squats

1. Stand with your feet just greater than shoulder-width apart.
2. Start the movement at the hip joint. Push your hips backward and "sit back into a chair". Make your hips go back as far as possible.
3. Squat as deep as possible, but keep your low back tensed in a neutral position.
4. Don't let your lower back become rounded.
5. Push with your glutes, hamstrings, and quadriceps to return to the start position.

Incline Pushup

1. Keep the abs braced and body in a straight line from toes (knees) to shoulders.

2. Place the hands on a chair, counter or other stable elevated object, hands slightly wider than shoulder-width apart.

3. Take 5 seconds to lower yourself down until you are 2 inches from the counter or chair.

4. Push through your chest, shoulders and triceps to return to the start position.

5. Keep your body in a straight line at all times.

Plank

1. Lie on your stomach on a mat.

2. Raise your body in a straight line and rest your bodyweight on your elbows and toes so that your body hovers over the mat.

3. Keep your back straight and your hips up. Hold (brace) your abs tight. Contract them as if someone was about to punch you in the stomach, but breath normally.

4. Hold this position for the recommended amount of time.

Lying 1-Leg Hip Extension

1. Muscles: Butt, hamstrings (back of thighs)

2. Lie on your back with your knees bent and feet flat on the floor.

3. Brace your abs, and contract your right glute (butt muscle) while you take your right leg, lift it off the floor and hold it in the position shown.

4. Using the left glute, bridge your hips up.

5. Keep your abs braced. Do not use your low back to do this exercise.

6. Slowly lower your hips down until they are an inch above the ground.

7. Perform all reps for one leg and then switch sides.

Ball Cobra

1. Lie with ball under mid-section; feet pointed toward floor and legs straight.

2. Extend arms in front of ball.

3. Draw-in belly button and squeeze butt muscles.

4. Pinch shoulder blades back and down to bring arms around to side of body.

5. Return arms to front of body.

Wall Squat

1. Stand against a wall with your feet just greater than shoulder-width apart.

2. Place your feet 12-18 inches in front of the wall.

3. Start the movement at the hip joint. Lower your hips down until your thighs are parallel to the floor.

4. Push with your glutes, hamstrings, and quadriceps to return to the start position.

Jack Knife (stability ball)

Muscles: Abs, rectus femoris (quadriceps, front of thighs)

1. Brace your abs. Put your elbows on the bench and rest your shins on the ball.

2. With your arms straight and your back flat, your body should form a straight line

3. from your shoulders to your ankles. Hold that position for 3 seconds.

4. Keeping your back straight (don't round it), slowly roll the ball as close to your chest as possible by contracting your abs and pulling it forward.

5. Pause briefly and then return the ball to the starting position by rolling it backward.

6. Hold the extended position for 3 seconds and repeat.

Squat Thrusts with Pushup

1. Start in the top of the pushup position with your abs braced.

2. Perform a pushup. Return to top position.

3. Thrust your knees in towards your chest and then back out quickly.

4. Repeat.

224

Stretch & Recovery

Exercises are listed in the order you perform them during the workout for your ease of use.

Three Plane Neck

1. Slowly turn head left, then right, gradually increasing range of motion.

2. Tuck your chin in, then tilt your head back.

3. Tilt your head strictly to one side, then to the other (no twisting).

Tip: Perform this movement in a slow, controlled manner. Do not combine the 3 movements into a head roll.

Shoulder Circles

1. Draw circles with your shoulders, as big as possible.

2. Inhale & expand ribcage as shoulders are moving back.

3. Do 10 circles one direction, then switch directions and do 10 more.

231

Fist Exercise

1. Extend fingers from closed fist, then clench your fist again.

2. Perform a total of 20 repetitions

Tip: Try to perform this movement as quickly as possible.

Wrist Rotations

1. Sit on a bench or other surface and hold a dumbbell by the end.

2. Brace the elbow of the arm that is holding the weight against your thigh.

3. With your opposite hand, hold firmly against your thigh the wrist of the hand that is holding the weight.

4. Lower the weigh to one side, rotating at the wrist. Slowly rotate your wrist to the other side. This is one repetition.

5. It will be tempting to move the elbow; limit the movement to your wrist and forearm.

Elbow Circles

1. Make circles with your elbow maximally bending and straightening it out.

2. Outward circles are more awkward than inward ones.

3. Elbow circles are also great for your shoulders.

Egyptian

1. Start with arms out straight and your palms facing down.

2. Pivot and turn to one side while keeping your arms in the same spot in space.

3. Both hands should turn up as much as possible.

4. Switch sides keeping your shoulders in line.

Arm Circles

1. Draw maximal circles with one or both arms.

2. Repeat in opposite direction.

Hula Hoop

1. Imitate a hoola hoop motion.

2. Keep shoulders stationary and make big circles with your hips.

Ankle Circles

1. Draw circles with your toes while making a point of achieving a maximal range of motion in ankle.

2. Pointed toes, toes to nose, and in and out motion.

Knee Circles

1. Place your hands above your knees – not on
    kneecaps.

2. Make small circles, NOT large.

Tip: Knee was designed for only minimal lateral motion, so
keep your circles tight and small.

Toe Hang

1. Stand straight up with legs together.

2. Slowly bend forward as far as it is comfortable.

3. Keep knees locked or close to it.

4. Keep your head down and do not look up.

5. Squeeze glutes hard and breath in deep.

6. Relax and let out breath and sink deeper in to hang.

Cobra

1. Lie prone on the floor. Stretch your legs back, tops of the feet on the floor. Spread your hands on the floor under your shoulders. Hug the elbows back into your body.

2. Press the tops of the feet and thighs and the pubis firmly into the floor.

3. On an inhalation, begin to straighten the arms to lift the chest off the floor, going only to the height at which you can maintain a connection through your pubis to your legs. Press the tailbone toward the pubis and lift the pubis toward the navel. Narrow the hip points. Firm but don't harden the buttocks.

4. Firm the shoulder blades against the back, puffing the side ribs forward. Lift through the top of the sternum but avoid pushing the front ribs forward,

which only hardens the lower back. Distribute the backbend evenly throughout the entire spine.

Spine Rotation w/Club

1. Sit in a chair with feet & hips planted solidly.

2. Slowly turn your trunk clockwise and counterclockwise.

3. Make sure your head moves with your torso.

Head Turner

1. Sit in a chair facing forward. Turn your head to the left or the right as long as you can. Do not tilt your head, just rotate.

2. Apply pressure against your head with hand. Hold and allow tension to release.

3. Perform drill in both directions.

Headache Buster

1. Great for alleviating tension that can cause headaches.

2. Turn your head a little to the right as if trying to touch your chin to your collarbone.

3. On the side you have moved your chin, take that same side arm and grasp your head and pull in to your collarbone.

4. Allow the tension to release and repeat on other side.

Chest Stretch 1

1. Stand next to a doorframe. Raise elbow to shoulder height and rotate arm so that your hand is up (as if in a throwing position with elbow in line with your shoulder).

2. Press your elbow against the doorframe and slowly and gently rotate your upper body away from your elbow. Feel the stretch across the front of your shoulder and chest.

3. Hold for 30 seconds and then repeat for the other side.

Chest Stretch 2

1. Stand with your arm out-stretched and hand pressed against a wall or support.

2. Rotate your hips and feet away from your arm, to increase the stretch felt across the chest muscle.

3. Hold that position for 20 seconds and then repeat for the other side.

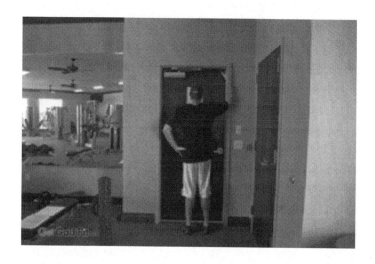

Shoulder Stretch

1. Raise your arm to shoulder height and bring your arm across the front of your body.

2. If using your right arm, your right hand should rest at your left shoulder.

3. Take your left arm and place it behind your right elbow. Slowly and gently apply pressure just above

your right elbow to feel a stretch in the back of the right shoulder.

4.   Hold for 30 seconds and then repeat for the other side.

Backswing Angel

1. Place the roller along the spine from the base of the skull to the tail bone. The knees should be bent and feet flat on floor.

2. Allow your pelvis and shoulders to roll in opposite directions on the roller.

Wrist Flexion

1. If you have wrist issues, this one can really help relieve some stress.

2. Get down on your knees and place your hans in front of you, pointing towards you as much as possible.

3. Keep elbows locked and gently shift weight towards hands until you feel the pull on the inside of your forearms.

4. Hold and let tension ease.

5. The angle between your arms will increase when you have released the tension.

Trunk Rotation

1.   Sit on a chair facing forward.

2.   Solidly plant your feet to anchor hips.

3.   Open your chest and turn your torso around your spine. Hold on to chair.

4.   Contract your muscles and breath deep.

5. Release tension and breath and twist a bit further.

6. Repeat on opposite side.

Kneeling Hip Flexor

1. Tight hip flexors cause bad backs, monkey butts, and athletic inferiority.

2. When flexors are tight, they do not allow your glutes (strongest muscle in the body) to exert themselves efficiently. Kneel on floor and face forward.

3. Torso and front shin should remain upright for the duration of the stretch and hips should remain squared.

4. Flex your abs to protect your back.

5. Once the tension is released you will begin to sag down.

Let's take this a step further so you can see how this can impact your backswing.

1. Leaning forward, place your hands on your knee not letting your knee drift forward.

2. Begin to twist and look out, do not look down.

Piriformis Stretch

1. Cross one leg in front of your body on the floor.

2. Lean your chest over the top of your front leg while you sit back on your hips.

3. Straighten out your back leg and bring it across your body to increase the stretch.

264

Seated Groin Stretch

1. Sit with your knees bent and feet together in a criss-cross fashion.

2. Gently press the tops of the knees down toward the floor with your elbows.

3. Stop when a slight stretch is felt.

Downward Facing Dog

1. Really focus on calf muscles and try to get heels to touch floor. This may take time, but is integral in helping to create more power, length, and tension in your swing.

2. Come to your hands and knees with the wrists underneath the shoulders and the knees underneath the hips.

3. Curl the toes under and push back raising the hips and straightening the legs.

4. Spread the fingers and ground down from the forearms into the fingertips.

5. Outwardly rotate the upper arms broadening the collarbones.

6. Let the head hang, move the shoulder blades away from the ears towards the hips.

7. Engage the quadriceps strongly to take the weight off the arms, making this a resting pose.

8. Rotate the thighs inward, keep the tail high and sink your heels towards the floor.

What should you do next?

Q: So I've finished the Shed Pounds to Shave Strokes workouts, what other workout programs do you have?

Answer:

Golf Fitness: 30 Yards or More in 30 Days or Less

30 Yards or More in 30 Days or Less is the workout to do AFTER Shed Pounds to Shave Strokes. This more advanced program to begin immediately after Shed Pounds is our core strengthening and power workout program.

This 4-week (advanced) to 8-week (Intermediate and beginner) workout program is designed to build on the base you create in Shed Pounds to Shave Strokes. In a nutshell, this is a tour pro caliber workout designed to improve golf performance and provide you with more distance, stamina, and control.

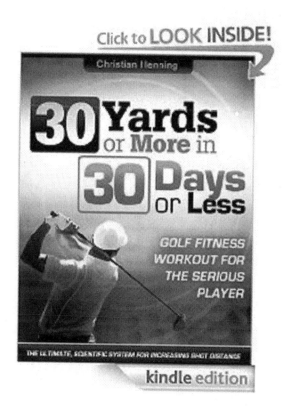

Get Your Copy Here: ==> http://golff.it/30in30

- Build Balance, Flexibility, Strength, and Power in just 30 days
- Dumbbells, Stability Ball, and a Chair are all you need.
- Beginner, Intermediate, and Advanced Workouts included.

What is my mission?

My Mission: To help 1 million golfers by the year 2020 to improve their health and play the greatest game of them all longer.

Aid in eliminating pain and injuries, improve their golf game through improved performance and consistency, and live longer so they can comfortably play golf in to their golden years.

What has inspired me to help 1 million men and women transform their lives?

Like many Americans, bad health has taken many loved ones way to early that were close to me. Both my mother and father died in their early 60's. Smokers... who regularly ate fast food.. and cooked dinners using a deep fryer... and rarely exercised.

Even my grandfather passed away too soon in his early 70's.

Growing up, Thursday was when my dad, grandfather and I would go play golf together. My dad was decent and could hit the ball a long way.. my grandfather was like Yoda with a sand iron. He was even short like Yoda. :)

The matches were competitive but most of all - fun.

I'll never forget those days and I wish they could have gone on forever. The matches ended before they had to. Bad health took my two favorite golfing buddies from me.

Sad – and preventable, to a point.

We all die some day. However, you can extend your life by adopting some daily rituals.. Rituals that take a small fraction of time each day... but lend years to the end of your life. I'm a firm believer that taking care of yourself all of your life will help you age gracefully in your golden years. Mom, dad, and my grandpa didn't take care of themselves as well as they could have.

Who knows how many years we lost together due to the bad choices they made concerning food and exercise?

I was alone.

No one close enough to me to ask for advice when I needed a fathers advice.. or a grandfathers.. or a mothers. No one to see the accomplishments I would rise to. No one to help when the days were dark.

Yes, It Can Happen To Anyone...

Most of my life I have been physically active and taken reasonable care of myself – however – I did go through a five year span in a corporate environment where I literally 'let myself go'. Soon after my mom passed away I quit my job as an assistant pro at a golf course.. to get a real job.

I had a child on the way and could no longer get by "having fun" on the golf course. Within a few years in the corporate world I discovered I was on the same path as my parents.

Bad habits soon developed as I tried to fit in to the corporate culture.

My weight ballooned up to 245 pounds. Prior to the corporate job, my weight fluctuated between 195 and 205 pounds.

Gone were the days of golfing from morning to night and being physically active. My new destiny appeared to be a wobbly chair under fluorescent lighting. I was miserable not only physically, but mentally.

I hated my situation. Kept away from the game I loved so much and trapped in an office…

Days and weeks went by without touching a golf club. My 'touch' soon followed and I became scared to even play a round of golf. If I did play, I knew the result would be depressing. Invited to play golf with friends, I would always decline. Embarrassed of how I looked and how far I had fallen athletically.

Going from a scratch golfer to someone who couldn't break 90 was a tough pill to swallow.

Even more difficult was the image I would see in the mirror. My muscular body shrouded with pounds of unwanted fat. Muscles that had lost their tone and disappeared. A few years after working in misery, I decided to finally play golf with some of my co-workers and realized my distance and my game were totally gone. I used to CRUSH the ball and out-drive just about anyone.

No longer.

I went back home.. embarrassed and ashamed.

How could I let myself go this far? I had gained 45 pounds of pure lard! I could barely walk up a flight of stairs without getting out of breath. My eating habits were relegated to drive-through windows and fast food establishments. My job was unfulfilling.

Ridiculous!

One day, I decided enough was enough. I was first going to get back my health, and second, get back my golf game. The third step would be to regain financial control of my situation.

Let me tell you, it was tough. Mentally it was as hard as anything I have ever done.

It took five years of dedicated effort to reverse the five years of 'lardiness' (my word for laziness and adding poundage).

Five years to build my lardiness, five years to take it off.

Think about that for a second... five years... Please understand this process can take awhile. Losing that fat and regaining my game were worth the five years of effort.

Maybe the weight loss was a bit slow and it didn't melt off like it does with some folks.. but I gained experience and knowledge that help me connect with people who are like I was... people that need my help.

I learned that playing golf and fitness both made me happy. Once my health was back, my golf game was in check. My joy for the game increased.

My distance was back, albeit with a new twist – I could hit it even further! In addition, my self confidence surged. I felt great about who I was and how I arrived there.

Along my journey I became a certified personal trainer, read countless books and journals, and watched tons of DVD's. And what about the job I hated? I quit and started three businesses I own, of which I still run two today. Five short years I transformed my entire life from the inside out.

Golf, fitness, and running my own businesses are my daily rituals now.

The inspiration to help 1 million women and men to transform their lives is simple... it's about helping others spend Thursday afternoon with their father and grandfather.

Legal Disclaimer

You must get your physician's approval before beginning this exercise program. These recommendations are not medical guidelines but are for educational purposes only. You must consult your physician prior to starting this program or if you have any medical condition or injury that contraindicates physical activity. This program is designed for healthy individuals 18 years and older only.

The information in this report is meant to supplement, not replace, proper exercise training. All forms of exercise pose some inherent risks. The editors and publishers advise readers to take full responsibility for their safety and know their limits. Before practicing the exercises in this book, be sure that your equipment is maintained, and do not take risks beyond your level of experience, aptitude, training and fitness. The exercises and dietary programs in this book are not intended as a substitute for any exercise routine or treatment or dietary regimen that may have been prescribed by your physician.

Don't lift heavy weights if you are alone, inexperienced, injured, or fatigued. Don't perform any exercise unless you have been shown the proper technique by a certified personal trainer or certified strength and conditioning specialist. Always ask for instruction and assistance when lifting. Don't perform any exercise without proper instruction. Always do a warm-up prior to strength training and interval training.

See your physician before starting any exercise or nutrition program. If you are taking any medications, you must talk to your physician before starting any exercise program, including Shed Pounds to Shave Strokes or 30 Yards or More in 30 Days or Less. If you experience any lightheadedness, dizziness, or shortness of breath while exercising, stop the movement and consult a physician.

You must have a complete physical examination if you are sedentary, if you have high cholesterol, high blood pressure, or diabetes, if you are overweight, or if you are over 30 years old. Please discuss all nutritional changes with your physician or a registered dietician. If your physician recommends that you don't use Golf Fitness: Shed Pounds to Shave Strokes, please follow your doctor's orders.

Made in the USA
San Bernardino, CA
28 September 2018